The Working Woman

The
Working Woman
A Handbook

BY NIKI SCOTT

SHEED ANDREWS AND MCMEEL, INC.
SUBSIDIARY OF UNIVERSAL PRESS SYNDICATE
KANSAS CITY

Library of Congress Cataloging in Publication Data

Scott, Niki.
  The working woman.

  1. Women — Employment — United
States.   2. Mothers — Employment — United
States. I. Title.
HD6095.S4   331.4'0973   77-22023
ISBN 0-8362-0733-5
ISBN 0-8362-0745-9 ppb.

To Chuck Scott-Henderson, my husband,
who believed in me long before I did

CONTENTS

PART IV

Introduction

This book is different. It won't give you fast, pat answers to the problems working women face each day. It will not give you the perfect reply to the married boss who has been asking you out to dinner. It will not tell you exactly what to say to your husband, who expects you to do all that a housewife does and work fulltime, too. It will not stop you from sometimes feeling guilty and inadequate if you're trying to be a wife, mother and career woman. Nothing can do those things. They go with the territory.

What I hope this book will do is give you a close look at how other working women are coping with their problems. You'll discover you're not the only one who is filled with rage when you're treated unfairly in the office. You'll learn that other wives are exhausted (and resentful) because their husbands still think of housework and child-rearing as "woman's work." Or because their husbands will "help out"—but refuse to assume responsibility around the house. And, if you're single, you'll find that your sometimes crushing loneliness is universal— "swinging" singles live, for the most part, only on the pages of those glossy magazines we can't seem to resist reading.

No one can tell you exactly what to say or do about the specific problems you face as a working woman. Each of us must find her own answers; learn what works and what doesn't for us. But just knowing you're not the only one—knowing your counterparts in Dallas and New York and Appleton, Wisconsin, are going through it, too, can help enormously.

When you finish this book, you will know absolutely that you are not alone. You are not the only one whc

overreacts from time to time, who wants to be more assertive, who fears success as much as failure, who sometimes
wonders if it's all worth it, and sometimes secretly longs
for the days when a woman's role was clearly defined—
when being a good wife and mother was enough. Nor are
you the only woman who loves her job and who feels
guilty because she does.

That's what the *Working Woman* is all about—sharing,
learning and growing together. In the course of writing it,
I have heard from and talked to men and women of all
ages, married and single, living in small towns and large
cities, from the Pacific coast to the Eastern seaboard,
working in factories, offices and executive suites.

I have seen women struggling with incredible
burdens—rearing children alone, supporting aged parents, struggling with loneliness and self-doubt, managing
two full-time jobs (one at work and another at home) and
being treated like beasts of burden in both places. Generally, they cope with quiet courage—underpaid, unrecognized and unrewarded. I am constantly awed by the
strength and determination of our so-called "weaker sex."

Every working woman I know deals with conflict in
some area of her life. It can exist between husband and
wife, parent and child; it can be with your boss, or your
mother, or a neighbor—but it's there. And most of all, it
is inside us.

Many of us grew up believing we would marry our
Prince Charming, have children, keep house, and
then . . . and then what? And then (if we were "normal")
we would be fulfilled simply by being good wives and
mothers and housekeepers. We would leave one Daddy
for another man—still sheltered, supported and cared
for. Now, with great pain and many doubts, we have
given up that eternal childhood to become independent,

contributing citizens.

In 1976 the Federal Bureau of Labor Statistics changed its definition of a "typical" American family to include a mother, as well as a father, working outside the home. Not only are half the women in this country working, but more than half of all mothers with children between the ages of six and seventeen work away from home—as do over 40 percent of those with preschool children, a figure that has nearly tripled since 1950.

More often than not, we do not work because we choose to. Three-fifths of this country's working women are single, widowed, divorced, or married to men who earn less than $7,000 a year—an income no longer adequate to support a family of four even modestly. These women didn't take off their aprons one day and flounce off to the office. They work because they must.

With spiraling costs and ever-present inflation, the days of the traditional, one-income family are numbered. The U.S. Department of Labor estimates that 92 percent of those women who are now of college age will work sometime during their lives. These young women may well be better prepared than we were.

Marriages begun fifteen years ago, under an entirely different set of assumptions, are in trouble today. The old role models aren't relevant any more and husbands, as well as wives, are searching for new ones. The letters I receive from men ask, "What has happened to her? Why aren't we enough for her, any more? She seems so angry—what am I supposed to do? She only tells me what I shouldn't do!" The letters from wives say, "How can I get him to change, to understand? He says he will—but I'm still the one who is responsible for the children and the shopping and the housework even though I work as hard as he does all week!"

I do believe that most men are not ruthless, selfish, chauvinistic people. They are, rather, confused, threatened, insecure, sometimes angry and mostly scared. They want to be fair—but they're not sure what "fair" is. Nothing in their childhoods prepared them for this rapid change, either. They assumed they would marry, have children, and support their families. They assumed their wives would take care of the house and children (happily) while they concentrated on "getting ahead."

The roles for men and women had been clearly defined, by their parents. Mom was happy (everyone assumed) just being a wife and mother—and Dad was happy (apparently) earning a living. Boys were taught to be assertive and goal-oriented; girls were taught to be soft and gentle. Men had careers; women had babies. It was all so simple!

Now, their wives are going to work. Treated as adults in the business world, they expect to be treated that way at home. Suddenly we're saying "no" to another baby, and "yes" to a life of our own. We're asking for equal participation in all aspects of our marriages—demanding an equal "say" in the decision-making and equal sharing of household chores and child-rearing. We're saying, "I will work, because I want to and because one income is no longer enough. But, in return, you must assume your share of responsibility at home." Now and then some of us are saying, "Fix your own damned eggs. I have to get to the office!"

Wrote one man, married just three years, "I don't know where I fit. She can work, but I can't have babies. If I could, I would. But I can't. All I can do is work to support them and help raise them when I'm home. Now she says she doesn't want children! Where does that leave me?"

In a state of conflict—no doubt about it. And it leaves most women in the same state. The women's liberation movement tells us how things *should* be, how relationships *should* work, how people *should* be allowed to grow and change in equal partnerships. But something has been missing, I think, and that is help with the way things are while we're waiting for them to be as they should be. That, too, is what this book is all about.

The man you married six, or twelve or twenty years ago (and still love) isn't going to change overnight—no matter how many copies of *Ms.* magazine you force him to read. Employers are not going to treat you fairly until they are forced (slowly) to do so. Child-care problems for working mothers are not going to be solved until this society recognizes that restructuring must occur to fill the needs of today's working parents.

In the meantime, we working women juggle full-time jobs, husbands (or boyfriends), children, household chores, errands, community work, social lives and our own feelings of inadequacy and anger. We give 400 percent of ourselves, every day. And we are, understandably, exhausted.

For the first time, we want it all. We want individuality, independence and jobs that fairly reflect our abilities. But we want marriage too; rose-covered-cottage fantasies are not at all a thing of the past—one need only visit college campuses to see that. And generally we want, or already have, children. Motherhood is still an assumption for most of us. (In "wanting it all," I must add, we want only what men have always had. No one asks a man if he plans to work or have children! It is assumed he can have both. No one asks him if he plans to give up his career when he marries, either—it is assumed he can have both.)

But I think all of us, deep down inside, have moments

xiii

of wondering if we're doing the right thing. There may be a working woman who doesn't—but I haven't met her. We wonder if we *can* have it all. Can we rear happy, secure, well-adjusted children, keep our marriages together and handle a full-time job, too? The answer, I believe, is "yes." But not (for a while) without conflict, guilt, doubt and constant self-examination. And not without time—to learn how to assert ourselves effectively, demand what is rightfully ours, give what is ours to give, and stop feeling inadequate because we cannot give all of ourselves, all of the time.

In the business world, as well as at home, we face enormous odds. The U.S. Department of Labor admits that the differential between male and female salaries has doubled in the past twenty years—and, they say, a "large part" of that differential is due to sex discrimination. In the South and in small towns that differential is staggering. In Mecklenburg County, North Carolina, for example, female college graduates, working full-time, earn less on the average than men working full-time with an eighth grade education. Further, the average income for male college graduates in that state was $14,223 in 1975. For female graduates it was $7,862.

We do face discrimination—without a doubt. The deck is stacked against us. Worse yet, we sometimes stack the deck! Most of us weren't groomed to be career successes. While the boys were playing football and joining the debating team—learning to compete, to be assertive, to plan ahead, to go after the ball, even if they lost once or twice—we were "dressing up" and playing with dolls.

Later, the boys were praised for standing up for themselves; their anger was rewarded because it was "manly," and "What are you going to be, when you grow up?" was a common question—while we were being taught not to compete too hard (except against each other for a man), or be too bright. And our anger was definitely not rewarded; it was "unladylike."

We still pay for that training. Most of us are just beginning to think in terms of career goals. We find it difficult to assert ourselves in a positive way—to ask for the raise we deserve or the promotion we've earned. We tend to sit back, work quietly and assume (hope) our abilities will be recognized, and our competence rewarded. All that may be ladylike, but it sure as hell isn't effective!

For us, the old role models are no longer relevant. Now we must ask each other for help and advice. We've begun to share, rather than compete. We are learning—to survive in the business world, take risks, set long-range career goals and accept responsibility for our successes as well as our failures.

In short, and at long last, we have begun to take ourselves seriously. Genes have nothing to do with this ability. It is not inherited by males—only learned. And taking ourselves seriously gives us the confidence to share our successes and failures. We *all* teach, as well as learn; each of us has a role model—whether we like it or not.

Now, finally, I am not afraid to say: You are my friend, not my enemy. We are growing and it's sometimes painful—but all growth is. You and I can share one another's pain, and rejoice in each other's achievements. You do not threaten me. In fact, my future unfolds with yours. Because we're all in this together.

PART I

Working Mothers

1

I Almost Failed That Night

It was a bad day—we all have them. This one was a classic, that got steadily worse hour by hour.

My car wouldn't start, the telephone rang incessantly, there was no time even to grab a sandwich for lunch, and by late afternoon my early-morning headache had become a throbbing monster.

Drained by 5:30 P.M., with still so much to do, I barely went through the motions of dinner at home.

To my twelve-year-old, it was: "Pick up your books. Why do you always leave them there?"

And: "Later—I'll help you with your homework later. Can't you see I'm busy?"

Then, to my eight-year-old son: "I know you're hungry! I'm fixing dinner as fast as I can, now don't bother me."

I seethed inside wondering when (ever?) I would be able to sit quietly and sort through the wreckage of this particularly "bad day."

Dinner finally was on the table. ("Wash your hands,"

"Pour the milk," "Come ON!"). They picked at their food, bickered back and forth—I barely heard them.

At last, dishes washed and a load of laundry started, it was time for baths and pajamas and (at last, at last) peace and quiet.

Then—the explosion!

With small fists clenched, John, the eight-year-old, stamped his foot and wailed, "No, I don't want to go to bed! It isn't time!"

All the anger, suppressed throughout the day, welled up. This eight-year-old, my son, defying me was the last straw. I started toward him—then stopped.

Something in his eyes—desperation, hurt, loneliness, betrayal—the look of a small, cornered animal standing his ground, stopped me.

"John . . . " Wary, fists still clenched, he waited. On my knees beside him, no longer towering over him, I held out my arms and he came into them, burrowing, his tears hot against my neck.

And then, haltingly, he told me about his day, and I listened—really listened—to what he had to say.

Two older boys had picked on him, on the playground that morning. Later, he had been accused by his teacher of something he hadn't done. He'd left his lunchbox on the school bus and had been embarrassed to tell anyone, so for lunch his best friend had donated a small bag of potato chips—that was all he had had to eat. ("Don't bother me," I had said, when he complained he was hungry.)

And one of his "friends" had told him he was going to "flunk" second grade, because he hadn't known the answer to an arithmetic problem. "I'm going to flunk, Mom.

4

He said so," John said, through his tears and his fear.

Silly? Of course, it was. This child, at the head of his class, isn't going to flunk anything.

Silly? Not when you're only eight and you haven't yet learned about envy and cruelty and what friendship is all about.

Small problems? He had had as bad a day as any adult could have had. Worse than my own.

And so I learned again from a small human being that children, even children of working mothers, are human beings with all the problems and worries and fears we have. And none of the defenses.

That's hard to remember, when we're trying to shift gears from one role to another at the end of the day. The demands on a working mother's time and energy are enormous—almost as great as the rewards, sometimes.

I almost failed that night, and I may fail again. *All* mothers, whether they work or not, fail from time to time.

But I hope I never forget the look in my son's eyes that night. I hope I never again forget that children can have "bad days" too.

Of course, there were other times, other days, when I was unable to respond immediately to my children's needs.

Sometimes their fantasies are as demanding as their troubles. My eldest son, on the threshold of adolescence, reminded me of just how easily children can blend doubts and fantasy. And he also reminded me that to children, what is real for them is often not what is real for adults.

One day, he wandered into the kitchen, slumped into a chair, and said nothing. Everything okay? "Yeah . . . I

5

guess." His eyes followed as I scurried about, home at last after a hectic day.

"Mom, do you think I'll ever go to the moon?"

"You might, someday. Would you set the table and call your brother? Oh, and on your way be sure and pick your books up. They're on the couch and the Cub Scouts are meeting here tonight."

Busy, my mind jumped from one chore to another. So much to be done—so little time each week. "Cub Scouts, tonight; get a sitter for Saturday night; we're almost out of clean clothes. There's office work to be done at home this weekend; the dog needs a distemper shot. . . ."

He hadn't moved.

"Bobby! I thought you were going to set the table and call your brother!"

"I am. But Mom . . . what if they've stopped going to the moon by the time I'm grown up? What if they're going somewhere else and it's so far away it would take years to get there?"

I counted to ten. Then whirled to face him.

"Aren't there enough things to worry about right here and now? What about tomorrow and next week? What about this dinner that's going to be cold if you don't set the table? And the twelve Cub Scouts who are going to arrive in forty-five minutes and find us still eating?"

He plunked silverware on the table, silently.

Later (was this day ever going to end?) he reappeared. "Mom? Are you busy? It's just. . .well. . ." He sat down, awkwardly.

"I wish we had more time to talk about things, Mom. Not big things, not just when something is wrong. We

6

used to just talk, you know? And sometimes we'd take a walk or read together or we'd just, well, talk. About things . . ."

"What things?" Clean clothes would have to wait.

"Like—you know—before dinner. About what if they're going farther than the moon when I'm old enough to go? I don't know what I'll do, Mom, because I'm going to be an astronaut and I'll have to go where they send me. But if they send me to Mars or even further it will take years to get there and years to get back and then . . . and then . . . ." He stopped for breath and swallowed hard.

"And then what?"

"Then I won't get to see you hardly at all. Any of you. I won't live here any more and I won't get to come home, even. And I don't know what I'm going to do about that.

"I just wish I didn't have to grow up at all, sometimes. I can't imagine having to live away from home and never seeing you and Dad. And everything."

It was my turn to swallow hard. We working mothers somehow find time for full-time jobs, and husbands, and children's problems, and laundry, and Cub Scouts, and shopping trips and friends, and housework.

It's finding time for nothing that is so difficult. Or something—like a thirteen-year-old who's much too old to be scared of much—except going to Mars and growing up.

It isn't enough to find time when there is a real problem. Unless I hear him, I may not know when there is one. Somehow, I must find more unscheduled time—to talk, to listen, to keep in touch.

7

2

"The Only Person Who Doesn't Want Children Is Me"

She assumed she would be a mother one day. Everyone did. She went to college, graduated with honors, fell in love with the "right" kind of man, and married.

Then she went to work.

"The job was going to be temporary—just for a few years until we could afford a house and furniture. Then I was supposed to get pregnant, quit my job, and stay home," she said.

"But I didn't know how much I'd love my job, when we made all those plans. And now it isn't just a job, it's a career and very important to me.

"I work hard, no doubt about it. But it's never boring and the people I work with are fun and interesting. The days pass so fast I can hardly believe it when the week is over."

Her husband wants children. Her mother wants grandchildren. His mother wants them, too. Their friends have

8

begun asking when they plan to "start a family."

"The only person who doesn't want them is me, and I'm the one who would be having them! Does that make me abnormal? Is there something wrong with me, because I enjoy the life I have and don't have this burning need to reproduce?" she said.

"I don't need a baby to fulfill me (my mother uses that word a lot) because my marriage, my job and social life and volunteer work are enough.

"But still, my husband thinks it would be nice to have children. He isn't adamant—hasn't resorted to ultimatums. Yet. But I know he wants them, and that would mean giving up a job that is very important to me."

She reached for a book of matches, then tore them out one by one as she talked.

"Look, if I had a routine job—one that bored me—it would be different. I'd welcome the chance to quit and stay home! It hasn't worked out that way—but how could I know that four years ago, when I'd just graduated from college and married Jim?" she said.

"I do not believe that little babies should be left with strangers; so I would feel obligated to stay home for a few years, at least.

"You can't just hop in and out of a career like that! Jim can't, either. But men don't have to choose between having children and having a career. It's easy for them to have both, because the world assumes they will," she said.

"Maybe not wanting children isn't fair to him. If his urge to have kids comes between us, I will let him go—let him find someone who's willing to have them. I love him;

9

I wouldn't deny him children, if they're that important to him.

"But I'm not willing to give up, or damage, my career and a life I enjoy to have children I don't really want. I will not pretend to be something I'm not—and I'm not cut out to be a mother.

"It used to be that women *had* to have kids, to prove they were real women, or something. Now? We have choices, supposedly. And I choose a different kind of life. It may not be the right choice, for others. But it is for me," she said.

"I wish I'd known all this, before we married. But I didn't, and I can't change that. All I can do, now, is find 'fulfillment' in a way that's right for me. And for me it is not by having babies. . . ."

For Elizabeth, however, the solution was not reached that easily. Her response was one of pain and indecision—an inability to choose between the demands of a challenging, rewarding career and the responsibilities and joys of being a full-time mother and wife.

When I met her two years ago, Elizabeth seemed to know exactly what she wanted from her career and was determined to achieve it.

A special education teacher at the time, she wanted an administrative position in a large school system. And, having just earned her second graduate degree while working full time, she seemed well on her way toward achieving that goal.

But between then and now, Elizabeth and her husband

decided to have a baby—now, all she knows is that she's confused and upset.

"It never crossed my mind I wouldn't go right back to work after the baby was born. My husband assumed I would, too; he said he'd never wanted anything but a career wife," she said.

She worked until just three weeks before Michael was born, and informed the school board she'd be back at work when he was six weeks old.

"I loved being pregnant, and I really looked forward to a little vacation for six weeks. I remember telling people how lucky I was that we waited to have children, because in this day and age you don't have to choose between having children and having a career." For the first of several times, she choked back tears.

Then, the words tumbled out. "My mother came to visit, when Michael was born. When I told her I was going right back to work, she cried! Can you believe that? 'Oh, no,' she said. 'You're *not* going to leave that tiny baby with a stranger!'

"Then, my husband's mother came. She said the same thing—only to Michael, so I could hear. 'My poor, precious baby . . . is Mama going to leave you all alone?' I cringed, every time she did it," Elizabeth said.

The neighbors and the people she used to work with, and even her friends, say the same things to her.

"They look at me as though I've lost my mind, then give Michael this pitying look. I feel as if I'm leaving him on the orphanage step."

Now, Elizabeth has doubts, too.

"It's one thing to say I'll go back to work when *the* baby

11

is six weeks old; it's another thing to say when *my* baby, Michael, is six weeks old," she said, looking down at the small, sleeping bundle in her arms.

"What if they're right? What if it really damages him in some way? I'd hate staying home for years—I hate it already. But I know no one can love him as much as I do.

"My husband encourages me to go back to work, but he doesn't understand how hard it is. You read all those articles about women who go right back to work and it sounds so easy—but it isn't, because I can't be sure it's the right decision.

I don't think any mother knows for sure if she has made the right decision in leaving her children to go to work—whether the children are six weeks, or six or sixteen years old.

But I suspect the answer, if there is one, doesn't come from relatives, or friends or neighbors. If it did, few of us working mothers would have made it to our first job interview.

I am not sure what Elizabeth will finally decide.

But as she left, still holding Michael, she said,"You're the first person, besides my husband, who hasn't made me feel like a freak because I love my baby but I want a life of my own, too."

These two women have shown two very common aspects of the problems working women face when confronted with the choice of career or home. Obviously, though, men too feel strongly about the question.

If a wife stays home, her husband might come home nightly to a discontented, frustrated spouse. If she does go to work, her husband then shares more in the household duties and the caring of the child and, quite possibly, the guilt working mothers often feel about their children.

I met one man at a party who gave me his reasonable side of the story. Not surprisingly, his wife's views were markedly different.

"Of course I don't want my wife to work! But I can't tell her that," he said. "I wouldn't tell you, if you hadn't promised to keep my name a secret."

We'll call him Don. He is a thirty-year-old executive with a master's degree. His wife works, too.

What Don had to say the night we met may disturb you. But I thought I'd pass it along anyway, because I have a feeling a lot of husbands (sadly enough) might say the same thing, given a chance.

"I don't want my wife to work because we have a three-year-old son. That's the only reason. While she works, Tommy stays at home with our housekeeper who is competent, reliable and quite pleasant.

"But she has a high-school education, and we are both college-educated. She is a member of the Catholic church. We are Protestants. She believes Tommy should be allowed cookies and candy between meals. We do not. She is not as concerned with teaching him self-reliance as we are. Nor with fostering his vocabulary," Don said.

"So we zip his jacket for him on weekends and hide the cookies. And we try not to correct him when he calls a colt a baby horse and a cat a kitty.

"That's all right, I suppose. It just isn't the way we would raise him. And we're his parents."

13

"My wife earns $12,500 a year. Our housekeeper earns $8,200. So I know she's not working for the money; she's working for her own, personal satisfaction. And I can't deny her that right—wouldn't want to.

"But I'm just not sure our son is getting a fair shake. I don't really believe anyone can be a better mother to him than my wife, that's all.

"When we decided to have a child, there was an assumption that my wife would stay home and take care of him—at least until he was old enough to be in school. Maybe that was an unfair assumption. But we *both* assumed it," he said.

"Now, she has changed her mind. Now, someone else is guiding him and influencing him. And that someone (in my opinion) doesn't measure up to his own mother.

"You ask why I don't stay home with Tommy? Because I earn a little more than twice what my wife earns. And we cannot afford to give up that salary. We have lived up to—and past—our income for too long.

"We'd have to sell our house and take a loss. We wouldn't be able to pay the bills we have. We'd be in serious financial trouble, in other words. Maybe that's my fault; but I can't very well reverse it all now," he said.

Why can't he say these things to his wife? She seems like a reasonable sort.

"Because I'd come across like a male chauvinist pig, that's why! Using our son as an excuse to keep her in the kitchen, where she belongs. That doesn't happen to be true. But that's how I'd sound.

"Philosophically, I am convinced that every woman should have the right to have a career and be a mother, if that's what she chooses. I'm also convinced my wife's

14

work is as important to her as mine is to me.

"And I guess no one can know for sure whether Tommy is better off with a working mother and a qualified housekeeper, or with a full-time mother at home," Don said.

"I worry about him, that's all. I wish she had waited a couple of years. But I will not say that to her. How can I? I love her. I want her to be happy."

And how does his wife respond?

"I wouldn't go back to being a housewife for anything in the world," she said. "I think our son, who's three years old, is better off now and I think our marriage is, too.

"I stayed home for two years after Tommy was born, and I was totally miserable. I think a lot of women are cut out to stay home. That's fine, but I'm not—and it took me too long to admit it," she said.

"I was so bored! And boring, too. I had no input, except from an infant and other women in the neighborhood. By the time I decided to go back to work, I was watching soap operas and reading magazines half the day.

"You can spend just so long playing with a two-year-old and cleaning a three-bedroom house, you know. Then what?

"My husband wishes I were home. He doesn't say so, but I know it. He thinks Tommy would be better off with a full-time mother," she said.

"Maybe he would be, if he'd been born to a different woman—one who didn't want a career, an identity, of her own. But he wasn't better off with me home all day. I know—I was there!

"My husband didn't see me at two o'clock in the after-

15

noon, when I wanted to scream (and did, sometimes) because I was so sick and tired of picking up the same toys, over and over, and hearing the same two-year-old chatter, and saying the same words and looking at the same four walls," she said, shaking her head and shrugging.

"He saw our house as a retreat after being in the outside world all day. I saw it as a prison. He thought taking care of Tommy would be interesting and rewarding—because he didn't have to do it all day.

"He was honestly surprised when I decided to go back to work—at a job I loved and was good at, before our son was born," she said.

"We were lucky. We found a warm, loving person to come to our house and take care of Tommy during the week. She seems to truly enjoy taking care of an active three-year-old. She may not do it exactly as we would, but Tommy is crazy about her! And that's what is really important.

"He's a healthy, happy little kid. He isn't neglected at all because I work. If I thought for a minute Tommy was suffering, I'd quit. But I don't. I see a little boy who gets lots of love and attention—from our housekeeper during the day, and from my husband and me at night.

"When I come home I'm honestly glad to see him. We spend more time taking walks and playing together than we did before I went to work—I'm sure of it. We enjoy each other now," she said.

"Frankly, I don't have much of a paycheck left by the time I pay our housekeeper. But in two years Tommy will be in school and my expenses will go down.

"In the meantime, I'm getting that much ahead in my

profession and earning enough for some luxuries we wouldn't have with just my husband's salary.

"More importantly, I'm a better mother, a better wife, and a much happier person. I believe firmly that doing what's good for me is good for Tommy, too.

"We don't have to make a choice between motherhood and having *some* life of our own, any more. Thank God for that! I could stay home for twenty years, if I had to. But I don't have to; that's the point.

"I have the best of both worlds now. Tommy does, too."

3

Choosing a Day-Care Center for Your Child

Is your child entering a day-care center or nursery this fall? If so, you're probably wondering how to tell if it's a good one.

There's no one way. But parents who have been through it—and child-care professionals as well—say there are some clues which may help you decide. You just have to know what to look for, they said (besides your state's stamp of approval).

"It isn't enough to ask questions—you have to snoop, play detective," the head of a nationwide chain of day-care centers said.

"I'd drop by unannounced, the first time. Try to get there around lunchtime (and check out the food your child will eat every day) or just before nap-time (when children are tired and at their worst) or first thing in the morning, while parents are dropping them off," she said.

"If the atmosphere is reasonably calm during those times, it probably is most of the time."

Once you get inside the center, teachers suggest you notice if the children are grouped according to age, so younger children are able to keep up.

Are the classrooms large enough to accommodate separate play areas—a doll corner, clay table, block corner and reading (or quiet) area, for instance? Are the children allowed to play where they like in the classroom during some portion of the day?

Is there a safe, outside play area where children can run off some energy in nice weather? Does it contain interesting, imaginative equipment, or typical (and boring) swings and slides?

"The answers to all those questions will tell a parent a lot about the center's attitude toward children," the head of a small center said.

And a conference with the center's personnel should tell you the rest.

"Make an appointment—and bring your child with you. If the staff ignores her, seems annoyed if she interrupts, or expects her to sit for an hour with nothing to do, you'll know even more about them," a day-care worker said.

During the interview, be honest! Parents, especially, were adamant about that. If you're a single parent, if you work long hours, if your child is shy, or has a rough time with new situations, tell them.

"Then watch their reactions. If they seem disinterested and bored, watch out. They may be later, too," a parent said.

Finally, parents suggested telephoning several parents whose children attend the center, asking if they're satisfied, how long their child has attended, how they view the center's program.

"Most parents don't mind a bit being called. You'll

learn more about the place and you'll get an impression of what kind of people send their children there. That can tell you a lot, right off the bat," said one veteran parent.

You've finally chosen the day-care center you like, and you worked hard to find it. You thought your child would love the one you finally picked. But it's been two weeks and he still clings to you, crying, when you try to leave him. Is it time to pull him out, make other arrangements?

Not necessarily, the experts say. In fact, one of the least important indicators would be whether or not he cries when you leave him.

"A lot of children resist being left by their working mothers. That doesn't necessarily mean they're unhappy while she is away—only that they would rather have her around, which is perfectly normal," a child psychologist said.

What *is* important is how your small son behaves when he comes home. If he clings, whines, demands, seems tense or constantly exhausted he (and you) may have a real problem.

Most children exhibit some of those symptoms for a while, as they adjust to a more structured, demanding day. But if a month goes by and the situation hasn't improved, you may want to have a conference with his teacher, the counselor said.

"Most children are extremely tired at night, when they first enter a group-care situation. They may be quite cranky, may fall asleep early or not be able to sleep, may have nightmares, even wet the bed occasionally because once asleep they're too tired to get up," he said.

"His teacher should know about any of these symptoms, and may be able to give some hints that will help. She's seen it all, don't forget."

Does your child talk about the center, his teacher, the other children? If not, it's time to do some careful questioning, he added.

"Ask him specific questions. Who is his favorite person at the center? Why? His least favorite person? Why? What's his favorite time of day? His least favorite? Why? You may get some informative answers that way.

"Then listen—really listen—to what he says. You can learn a lot," the counselor said.

If you've waited to give him time to adjust, done all you can at home, had a conference at the center and your child still seems unhappy, it may be time to make other arrangements.

"He may need more individual attention for another year, from a neighbor, relative or housekeeper," the psychologist said.

If individual care is out of the question, financially, you might try one other day-care center. Sometimes one sets a child off and another doesn't—though they look the same to us. And a personality clash with a particular teacher is quickly solved by switching centers, too.

Of course, before you even begin the chore of finding a day-care center for your child, you have to come to peace with yourself.

Is the care my child will get as good as what I can provide? Will the love be there? Will my child turn out all right after being in a day-care center?

21

I found one woman who is a firm believer in good day care. She is directing a day-care center and is convinced the children under her care are healthy, loving children.

She greets sixty-four children at the door every day. For more than nine hours she and her staff supervise, organize, stimulate and (hopefully) inspire these preschoolers, while their mothers work.

Originally from Sweden, she is the director of a private day-care center in the suburbs of New York City. If she could (and she can't) she would write a letter to each and every working mother who pays her forty dollars a week for child care.

In it, she would make the following observations:

"There are children here who have been with us since they were very small—infants, still. They do not know what it is to have anything but a mother who works. Their mothers have always worked.

"Most of the children who come here are happy individuals. A few are not. Yet all the mothers work. So what is the difference?

"It is in how Mama feels about her child, how she feels about working, how she feels about herself. These are the factors that determine a child's happiness, I think—not whether or not Mama works or stays home.

"If she is resentful about working (or Papa resents her job), that is going to come out, somehow. Generally, the children feel a great deal of it. These children are not happy. Naturally!

"If Mama isn't sure she's doing the right thing, children know that, too. These mothers who feel guilty make it up to the child in so many wrong ways.

22

"Sometimes they buy too many presents, they do not set reasonable limits at home (and enforce them) or they blame everything that goes wrong on the fact that they work—so the child never has to be responsible for his own actions. These children are unhappy, too.

"The children who are happy are very sure they are important to Mama, even though she works. They have breakfast (*very* important) and they are relaxed when they come in the morning. They hug their mothers or fathers goodbye. And they are hugged, too! No one is in such a hurry to be in the car and gone. . . .

"And in the evening they have time to talk a little bit, when they are picked up. They are not being rushed— pulled into their little coats and hurried right out of the door, always.

"These good parents are listening to those important things a child has to tell them. They are tired, yes; but not so tired they cannot be glad to see their child and hear about *his* day while they were away from him.

"On weekends, these parents spend time with their children. Not much, sometimes. It doesn't have to be much. But when the children come back on Monday morning, you will hear about shopping with father, or going to the library with mother, or to a movie or to the park—this and that they have done with their parents.

"Some of the children have nothing to tell, ever, because their parents spend no time with them. Often, these are unhappy children.

"Being a working mother's child is not so very different from being a housewife's child. I don't think so, anyway. If a child knows absolutely that he is important, if he has

23

faith that he is loved, he will probably be okay—here, or anywhere else.

"If he doesn't—if he feels underfoot and in the way—he will not be okay—here, or anywhere else. It doesn't take much time, really, to make a child know he is important. And it is absolutely crucial."

Which type of care is best for the child of a working mother? The answer depends—on you, your child's age and personality, your financial situation, and the city in which you live.

Many working parents just aren't comfortable leaving their child in a group-care situation all day. For them, hiring a woman to care for the child at home seems to be the best solution.

Child-care experts say there are some things you might keep in mind, however, when hiring a "mother substitute." And the first is that you forget that phrase altogether.

She isn't going to be a substitute mother. No one can be, really. She won't love your child as much as you do, won't worry about him the way you do, won't be as aware of every subtle nuance in his behavior.

All of which isn't necessarily bad. One mother is enough for any child! But if your expectations are realistic, both you and your child will have a much easier time adjusting to the person you do hire.

It is a good idea to make up a list of what you do expect —what you think your housekeeper's duties should be. Do you expect her to cook, clean, do the laundry as well as take care of your child?

The salary you can expect to pay for full-time help depends, again, on where you live. In large, metropolitan areas it can be as much as $125 a week, or more. In smaller cities, in the suburbs and in the South, salaries range from $70 to $100—and in all areas it's considered fair to pay for her transportation costs and her meals.

Be prepared, too, to pay her Social Security, give paid vacations each year and grant cost-of-living raises from time to time.

When hiring a person to care for your child it is absolutely essential that you ask for references covering at least the past three years, the experts say. Then check them—carefully.

The time it takes may save your child from being at the mercy of an alcoholic or a psychotic personality. Most women who seek such employment are mature, responsible, reliable people who perform a much-needed service. But it's worth checking to make sure you're not subjecting your child to one of the exceptions.

Once you've advertised, interviewed and checked references, you may be ready for a trial run—another good idea, experienced working parents say.

"Ask her to come for half a day, Saturday. And pay her, of course. Introduce her to your child, show her where things are—then watch," said one working mother.

"You can't tell everything, of course. But if she groans as she goes up the stairs, it she seems incapable of conversing with your child, or if she doesn't show up at all—you can move right on to the next name on the list."

Finally, once you've hired a housekeeper give her a chance. She isn't going to do everything just the way you do it, and it will take her a while to feel comfortable in your house, with your child.

"But if you have a strong feeling all is not well at home while you are at work, don't put up with it or be afraid to make a change," said one parent.

"It may mean a hassle for a while, until you finally find the right person. But it's more than worth it in terms of your child's well-being and your own, too."

4

Are Your Children Going to Camp?

If you haven't started stewing yet, you soon will. Summer vacation is coming, and with it a whole new set of problems for working mothers.

While your children look forward to lazy days, no school, time with friends, no school, swimming at the local lake or pool, no school, sleeping late and no school—you wonder what on earth you will do with them for three whole months while you work.

What you decide depends, of course, on where you live and what's available. If you're lucky, there are summer playschools, supervised pools and playgrounds, YMCA and YWCA camps, day-care centers with good summer programs and neighborhood-supported activity centers from which to choose.

The first thing to keep in mind, when considering a camp or group program, is safety, camp directors say. Every summer hundreds of children are injured because of overcrowding, poor equipment and lack of adult supervision.

27

"The laws vary from state to state—but be sure the program has your state's stamp of approval—that it at least meets minimum safety requirements," said a YMCA director in Maine.

"In my opinion, no adult should be responsible for more than fifteen youngsters under any circumstances, and no more than ten if the children are quite young or in the water," he added.

Speaking of water, many summer programs offer swimming. "Check to be sure an accredited lifeguard is on duty at all times, and that safety rules are strictly enforced. There are drowning and near-drowning incidents every year which just shouldn't happen," said a Red Cross representative.

"If a summer camp offers boating or canoeing, be sure life jackets are required at all times and that children in boats are accompanied by trained adults," a Coast Guard spokesman said.

Visit the camp or day-center, the experts advise. Talk to the director and several counselors, if possible. "And check to see what kind of training those counselors have," said one director.

"Too often high school students are employed by these camps with no prior training whatsoever. They are inexperienced babysitters at best, and should not be left in charge of ten to fifteen youngsters."

Are the children separated into age groups? "They should be—and four years' age difference is enough per group. Otherwise, you'll have bored older kids and little ones who can't keep up," a YWCA counselor said.

Finally, there should be time for quiet activity each

day. "A crafts room or corner, a reading area, a resting area for littler ones, a place to be calm and quiet—that's important, especially in the summer when children become overheated and exhausted if they run all day," one director said.

"After all, children are people, too. They need time just to be by themselves."

What if your children want to stay home this summer? They want to sleep late, see their friends, work on a hundred projects they've planned and generally "goof off."

If they're old enough to stay home alone all day, you'll set guidelines, make rules, post lists of chores and emergency telephone numbers—and worry a lot.

If they're younger, you are now in the market for a bright, pleasant, conscientious, eager, responsible person who will be a loving but firm companion to them until school starts again (finally) next September.

Good luck.

There are still, it seems, some college students around who enjoy children and want to earn a little money in the summertime. Not many—but some. The place to start is the nearest college or university. Most have employment placement offices, and all have bulletin boards.

It has been my experience that college students seldom visit offices of any kind—but they do read bulletin boards avidly. White index cards with a brief job description and your telephone number may turn up one or two candidates for the job.

If that fails, you might try your local high schools (hoping one or two seniors will need extra cash before heading for college in the fall), your YMCA and YWCA centers (they sometimes have a waiting list for camp counseling jobs) and your local newspaper.

If you do find a student who seems to want the job, the experts strongly advise you to ask for references, then check them—carefully. Talk to several teachers, if possible, or a school official; ask for names and telephone numbers of families who have employed the student as a sitter, and, finally, ask if you can meet with his or her parents. (We do most of these when we hire an adult, so why not when we hire a near-adult?)

If there are no students available, you might ask your state employment office if they have possible candidates for a temporary, though full-time job. Again, the experts say, check at least three recent references after you interview a potential summer housekeeper.

Still no luck? Often an ad in your local newspaper brings good results. Women who do not want to work all year might welcome a summer job at your house— especially if their older children are home to take care of their own younger ones, while they're working.

Finally, you might consider an arrangement with a stay-home friend or neighbor. If she has children of her own and enough space, she might welcome a summer playmate for her children and the chance to earn some extra money, as well.

There are both problems and advantages in such an arrangement, I think. The problems are: your child will not be in his own home; he or she may feel like the outsider; children who were the best of friends in June may tire of each other by August, and unless you and your at-home friend can communicate freely, you may not have a friend by September.

The advantages to such an arrangement are obvious. Your child will receive more individual attention than he would in a group situation; he or she will (hopefully) be in the neighborhood, if not at home, and able to see friends who live nearby; and (assuming they don't tire of one another too fast) your child is assured of having at least one playmate every day.

Whether you choose group care or individual care for your child this summer, perhaps the most important thing to keep in mind is this: School *will* start again, in September! It will . . . it will . . . it will. . . .

5

Now It's "Wait Until Mother Gets Home"

Not so long ago frantic mothers occasionally fell back on the old "wait 'til your father gets home" routine when driven to utter distraction by misbehaving youngsters.

Then, we learned that wasn't such a good idea after all. Delayed discipline only makes children anxious and guilt-ridden, we were told by the experts. And it makes fathers feel like ogres, as well.

So we stopped laying the heavy discipline on poor old Dad, home from the office after a rough day. We handled matters pretty much as they came up—until we went to work, that is.

Now, it's poor old Mom, home from the office after a rough day, who must be an ogre from time to time. It isn't any easier for her than it was for Dad.

"I would rather jump into a rattlesnake pit than play judge and executioner five minutes after I've come home from work. But it happens now and then and I just have to grit my teeth and be firm," said a reader, who works as a hospital receptionist, then comes home to four sons, eight to fourteen years old.

"With four boys in the house, there's a fair amount of disciplining that has to be done. I don't like it, my husband doesn't like it, but that's the way it is," she said.

"Obviously I can't do it if I'm not there, and neither can their father. So, if the need arises, we handle it together when we come home."

But this reader thinks there are some positive aspects to the situation, too.

"For one thing, I'm more likely to be fair and impartial just because I haven't been around them all day. I can be more calm and objective if I haven't listened to every squabble and witnessed every tiny transgression.

"For another thing, neither my husband nor I is the primary ogre; we share in the disciplining more than we did when I was home all day and Jim was at work. We talk it over more, too, because we are sharing it," she said.

"Then, too, we expect more of our children in terms of shouldering responsibility around the house. No one picks up after the boys; they're responsible for their own messes and that's good, I think.

"And all of them can cook just about as well as I can because they get dinner started every afternoon. I'm sure their wives are going to be glad I worked," she laughed.

But, despite those advantages, there are times when she wishes she hadn't come home at all.

"There have been nights when the kitchen is a mess, the boys haven't done their chores, they're fighting and yelling at the same time—those are the nights I'm tempted to just walk out again and not come back for several hours," she said, shaking her head.

"I'll tell you something—it isn't hard at all to discipline them when those nights come along. And I don't feel a bit like an ogre, either!"

There are times, though, when the problems won't wait until the end of the work day. Your children, alone at home after school, require disciplinary action immediately. And, as we know, we can't always take time from a work day to handle the situation.

One woman I know was forced to deal with the children repeatedly during her work hours. It didn't take long before she and her husband reached the boiling point.

She is a gentle person who seldom raises her voice. Her children seem bright, cooperative and well-behaved.

I told her so.

"Yes, but you didn't know them three years ago when I first went back to work," she said, shaking her head.

"What a year that was! They were nine and eleven years old, then, and didn't come home until 3:30 P.M. I left the office at 4:30 P.M., most days, and was home by five o'clock. For a while it worked like a charm.

"But about two months later everything began to fall apart. They'd always played well together, but suddenly they began to fight—over everything.

"Their father and I spent more and more time with them. We explained and talked and lectured and reassured them until we were blue in the face.

"It didn't help.

"We took away allowances, privileges, and sent them to

34

bed early. That didn't help, either," she said.

"We hired a college girl to come and stay with them— to referee. She lasted three weeks, then quit without notice. She told me she couldn't handle them, they wouldn't listen to a word she said.

"Every night we had a battle as soon as I walked through the door. Chores wouldn't be done, the house would look like a tornado had hit, and they'd be screaming and tattling on each other."

She considered quitting her job.

"But my husband talked me out of it. He said the girls were old enough to behave themselves for a little while in the afternoon, and that giving up wouldn't be right—for me or for them," she said.

"Then, the phone calls started. I'd look at the clock and know the phone would ring by 3:45 P.M. at the latest.

"First it would be one, then the other. 'She did this, Mom. Well, she said this. Mom, tell her to leave me alone. . . .' I wasn't getting any work done at all—and I was afraid to forbid them to call, because I didn't want them to feel out of touch with me.

"Sometimes they'd get on the extensions and out-yell each other. Pretty soon I'd be yelling too, and the whole office would know my children were home," she said, laughing.

"My sweet little girls had turned into absolute monsters!"

"Well, the day came when I had just had it. They called. There had been a fight. A lamp had been broken. Each said the other had done it.

"I got off the phone and told my boss I would have to be

out of the office for about an hour. I got in the car, drove home, walked into the house and marched them to their rooms," she said.

"Then I spanked them both—hard. I told them they were not to come out of their rooms until I came home, got in the car and went back to my office.

"That night my husband and I talked. Then we talked to the girls. We told them we would no longer tolerate such behavior and that we would take turns coming home every afternoon until it stopped.

"My husband said 'We are no longer interested in who did what. If you two cannot get along, stay away from each other. If you don't, if this fighting continues, one of us will come home. And if one of us has to leave the office, you can both expect a spanking—every time.'

"They didn't have much to say, and we wondered if we were being too rough on them. I felt terrible."

She paused, then grinned.

"I can't tell you exactly why, but that was the end of it. They went back to being normal kids. Oh, they argue now and then—all kids do. And the telephone rings from time to time, but not because of senseless, useless squabbling," she said.

"I think they needed to know I wasn't inaccessible— that I could come home. And would. More than that, I think they needed to know there were still firm guidelines operating here; that my working hadn't altered that.

"It wasn't the spanking that did it. It was showing them that I still loved them enough to stop them if they were on the wrong track; that they still came first," she said.

"Sometimes, discipline shows them that as much as a hug does."

If you're like me, we share some similar symptoms when the children are home, unattended. I suspect many working mothers show many of these same reactions.

If the telephone rings, you jump. If it doesn't ring, you worry. If you have to leave the office in the afternoon, you call home along the way.

There comes a time when our children are too old to be transported to a day-care center or baby sitter's house after school, but are not quite old enough to care for themselves at home (without a lot of worrying on our parts).

When does the time come? It depends on your city, your neighborhood situation and what your children are like.

But whenever it comes for you, be prepared for the following: you will worry, no matter how many safeguards you've established; if things go wrong, you'll feel guilty; if they don't, you'll still feel guilty—because Johnny can't have friends in after school, or because he's bored, or because you think he might be. If the children call too often while you're at work, you'll be annoyed; if they don't call, you'll worry.

And if you find a working mother who *doesn't* have any of those feelings, you're probably talking to someone whose mother lives a block away. In which case it's best to change the subject.

There are some steps we can take, however, to insure that the children are reasonably safe at home until we can get there. Compiled from interviews with family physicians, police officers and veteran working women, they are:

—If possible, ask a nonworking mother if your child can call on her, should there be a problem needing immediate attention.

—Be sure your child has your office telephone number and at least one other to call in an emergency.

—Brief children carefully on how to call the police department, should such a call be necessary.

—Instruct children to keep doors locked and not open them to strangers under any circumstances.

—Teach them not to tell strangers you are at work. They should simply say their mother will be home soon.

—Don't allow children younger than fourteen to cook anything unless you are in the house.

—Do not allow neighborhood children in the house while you are at work. The more children in the house, the more rambunctious they're likely to be—and accidents are more likely to occur.

Finally, working mothers suggested we keep our children as busy as possible, until we get home.

"Insist they do their homework in the afternoon—and give each child chores to do, too. It's a lot easier to keep kids out of trouble if they're busy," said one.

And a police officer added, "These safety rules may sound like just plain old common sense to you. But believe me, if more working mothers taught them to their kids there'd be a lot fewer kids hurt. We get the calls . . . we know."

6

"I Used to Be a Good Mother," But Now . . .

Jean is twenty-eight years old, works at a nondescript job downtown, lives in a trailer, is divorced and has two small children.

They stay home from school a lot.

Sometimes it's because her nine-year-old son doesn't want to go, and she has neither the time nor the energy to argue with him. Sometimes she is afraid teachers will notice certain things about the children and she keeps them home even if they want to go.

"I used to be a good mother—I was," she said, tearing a paper napkin into shreds while she lit cigarette after cigarette in the restaurant where we met to talk.

"When Don (her ex-husband) and I were together we did real good. I used to work part-time to help out with the bills and I kept the trailer clean and I was a real good mother.

"But now I just can't seem to do it the way I used to. I don't have any patience any more—the kids say one thing to me, and I'm ready to kill them! I didn't let Donny go to school because he whined at me over something and I slapped him. Across the face."

She covered her own face with her hands, for a minute, then said softly, "I can't even remember how it started that time. I had just come home from work and he started in, wantin' to know if he could do something I'd already said 'no' to."

That's how it usually starts, she said. Over nothing.

"I knew I was going to blow up, I was so tired, like I always am, and my feet hurt. I didn't know what I was going to fix for dinner and I told him to drop it, leave me alone. But he kept it up.

"I told him to go to his room and I walked in the kitchen and he followed me and I just blew up. I turned around and slapped him. As hard as I could."

Jean paused, then looked up for the first time and said, "It knocked him into the wall. I'm about twice as big as he is. He ran into his room and he was screaming and later, when he came out, there was this big red mark across the right side of his face, and the next mornin' it was black and blue. I kept him home and told him not to dare tell anyone or they'd come and take him away.

"And my little girl had marks on her legs from me spanking her with a belt about a week ago, and I kept her home because she didn't have no clothes but dresses to wear and I didn't want her teacher to notice the marks and ask a lot of questions," Jean said.

"When I get home at night I'm just wanting to sit down and not do a darned thing."

"Seems like the only way I can get them to leave me alone is to whip them. They'll just keep it up and keep it

40

up until I do. And sometimes, more and more lately, I'm so mad I can't stop, once I start."

Jean is afraid she will injure one of her children seriously, some day. She is afraid they will hate her as they grow older. She's afraid, too, that "someone" will try to take them from her if she doesn't take better care of them.

Jean is on the edge—not yet a brutally battering parent, perhaps, but filled with anger and likely to become one.

"It isn't really the children that make Jean angry, it's the situation in which she finds herself. It isn't so much the kids she's hitting, she's just hitting out—at something, anything."

So said psychologist Jack Walsh, staff member of a large mental health center in North Carolina, where Jean lives.

Lately, what used to be discipline has become near-battering, and Jean—guilt-ridden, angry, frightened—knows it.

"She's expecting far too much of herself. She's getting overwhelmed, and it's breaking through. I don't see any way she can stop it unless she can somehow find some breathing room for herself," said another psychologist, also practicing in Jean's home state.

"This kind of parent is more prevalent than you might think. Her behavior isn't extreme enough yet to be called battering, but there are so many, many parents who tread the line between what can be called discipline and what must be classed as violent behavior," he said.

Both counselors agreed Jean would benefit from counseling of some kind. And it is imperative that she somehow find time for herself, away from the children.

"She resents her job. One can assume she has swal-

41

lowed a great deal of anger toward her former husband who abandoned her, especially in the situation in which she now finds herself.

"With people bossing her around all day, her husband out of the picture entirely and no time to herself, that anger is going to come out—one way or another. She can't hit the unreasonable boss or her former husband, so she has nowhere else to go but to the kids. And they catch the brunt of a lot of emotion they can't begin to understand," Walsh said.

A third psychologist, who is female, said, "All working people, men and women, must be able to get away from time to time. This is especially true of working parents, and it's absolutely crucial for the single parent who has little or no respite from twenty-four-hour-a-day responsibilities.

"We take time out to eat—if we don't, we feel the physical effects before too long. There's a limit to our psychological energy, too. If we don't take the time for ourselves, if we don't renew ourselves, we are in a process of diminishing returns—and that's self-defeating," she said.

If pressure gets to you, from time to time, and you think it's affecting your relationship with your children, there are organizations in most cities which can help. Parents Anonymous is one. Contact and other twenty-four-hour hotlines can offer help, too, as can your family physician or local mental health facility.

If more parents had sought such help, last year, some of the more than 75,000 children who were officially classified as battered might have been saved.

Fortunately, Jean has agreed to do so.

7

"That's Okay, Mom. Have a Good Day"

"Mornings are important. They are the last opportunity for a working mother to touch base, before she and her children are separated for the day. They should be happy times for the whole family."

Ah, yes. Who could argue with that? A simple (but nourishing) breakfast, cheerful conversation, and off the little family goes—each member feeling secure and positive, able to tackle another day in the outside world.

There's just one problem: it generally doesn't work that way. Not in my house, and probably not in yours, either.

Most working women I know are tired and tense before they ever get to the office. And why not? Such a woman may have refereed at least two arguments, mopped up one glass of milk, stepped in two puddles of soggy cereal, murmured something reasonably pleasant to a sleepy husband and searched frantically for a sock, a mitten and one winter coat.

She has gulped a cup of coffee while doing the above, has nearly wrecked the car trying to comb her hair on the way to work, and gritted her teeth until her jaws ached so

43

as not to bellow at the top of her lungs and scare the family before the day even starts.

And that's on a good day.

Today, it was shoelaces—one broke. Then we learned the extra pair had been used as reins for the pet guinea pig—and soon I found myself sounding like a slightly deranged chipmunk, mumbling, squeaking and squawking while I looked for a shoelace, a piece of string, *anything* that might keep a tennis shoe on a small boy's foot for one day.

The ride to school was understandably quiet. The child with the yellow twist-tie in his tennis shoe seemed absorbed in a spot of dust on his notebook. I was absorbed in driving, combing and scolding myself—all at the same time.

"Honey, I'm sorry I was so upset. We were late, but that's no excuse. We'll get some shoelaces tonight."

He smiled, gave the twist-tie an extra tug and said, all in one breath, "That's okay, Mom. Have a good day. There's Danny, my friend. See ya."

Danny was climbing out of his car—and so was Danny's mother. Wearing a housecoat and slippers, she stood with a hand on her hip.

"You can clean up the mess when you get home. I don't know what's the matter with you! How could you lose a coat, tell me that!" Her voice carried across the parking lot.

And I saw on her face the same look I must have had on mine, earlier.

It isn't just because I work—nonworking mothers have morning horrors, too! And she feels as guilty as I.

Mornings are important—whether or not we work. But

when the working-mama guilties threaten us, it helps to remember nonworking mothers have them, too.

They may even sound like slightly deranged chipmunks from time to time. Danny's mother certainly did.

It's comforting to think many of us share the too-hectic morning routine. It took Danny's mother to remind me of that. Another mother, at another time, helped me get through a day I was sure I wouldn't get through. The scene may sound familiar to you.

He says he doesn't feel well. His stomach hurts (kind of), his throat is sore (a little) and his head hurts (now and then).

A healthy appetite, no fever, no visible symptoms of any kind. Just a small boy, looking smaller against the white pillow, who says he doesn't feel well.

Could he get up and dress? "Not really, Mom." He holds his stomach and moans, softly.

So, because he is only nine, and he might just be coming down with something awful, I call the office and give them the bad news.

He plays with books and puzzles and a radio and a game. I take his temperature, bring him lots of liquids and worry about the work piling up at the office.

By lunchtime he feels better. By 3:30 P.M. he feels much better. And an hour later he announces that he might be up to a quick football game in the backyard.

I could kill him.

Again, he says he doesn't feel well. This time, I'm ready. No fever, no visible symptoms—I am determinedly cheerful, sure he'll feel better once he gets to school.

45

I was nine once too, after all, and given to mysterious stomachaches now and then, when school was the last place I wanted to be.

The call comes from the school nurse early that afternoon. He has vomited and is running a fever. Could I come and get him? The guilt is massive, the remorse intense.

It's the flu. For two days he is subjected to intensive care. I'm there every minute, assuring him of how much he is loved, how sorry I am that he was sick at school, how glad I am that he's recovering nicely.

He seems a bit bewildered by all the attention.

A neighbor arrives for coffee on the second day. "You look pretty haggard. Is he seriously ill? I thought it was just a virus," she says.

The story of how "that poor little boy went to school sick because I was worried about my job" poured out—complete with tears.

She listened carefully, then smiled and shook her head. "Honey, we all do that. I sent my daughter to school with chicken pox last winter. Infected more than half the class! And I wasn't worried about a job, because I don't work," she said.

"I just thought she was faking—most kids do, occasionally. But I was wrong. Sometimes I keep her home and I'm wrong. All I can do is make the best decision possible with the information I have, which is exactly what you did."

The next day, I told a coworker what had happened. She threw up her hands and laughed.

"Of course! You can't win. If I keep my ten-year-old

home, she's sure to be well by lunch time. If I get tough and send her to school, I can just bet she'll be really sick," she said.

"I don't think it's because we work, though, although we can't stay home unnecessarily so we tend to lean a bit toward being tough. But I'm not so sure that's bad, either.

"My kids know that if they stay home, they'd better be really sick. I can't cater to them, go along with them just because they want to drop out for a day," she said.

"And that's pretty good training, I think. After all, the world won't cater to them either, once they're grown."

8

"I Feel More and More Defensive about Staying Home"

There are some working women we haven't talked about yet. They labor more than forty hours a week without benefit of minimum wage laws, retirement funds, Social Security payments, paid vacation time, raises or promotions.

They are housewives, homemakers, full-time wives and mothers—and theirs is a backbreaking job, filled with repetition and drudgery, which goes largely unrewarded and unrecognized.

Their only payment is the satisfaction of watching children grow healthy and secure, and in the knowledge that because of them households run smoothly and husbands find a welcome haven at the end of the day.

I know. I was one, for nearly ten years.

It is a full-time wife and mother (generally) who volunteers to chauffer *our* children to a school picnic, bakes cookies for our child's Sunday school party, works at the

PTA and the church bazaar and is the community fund-raiser.

In any community, it is the women who work full time at home who also provide the extra services we all need and appreciate. Without these volunteers, hospitals would be more understaffed, community centers would be nonexistent, educational and recreational programs would not be available.

And I know of few employed women who have not, at one time or another, called on a full-time homemaker for help. It's the friend who works at home we call on when a child is hurt or sick or needs help. She's the friend who "keeps the lid on" until we can get there.

"I feel more and more defensive about staying home. When Bill and I go to a party I'm always being asked what I do. And I find myself being apologetic about being 'just a housewife,' " a friend of mine said, not long ago.

This woman "does" more, in terms of sheer hard work, than any other working woman I know. She cares for three small children, a large house and a harried husband.

She is a full-time hostess, nurse, counselor, financial expert, gardener, maid, cook, chauffeur and a source of warmth, love and acceptance for her family, friends and the children she volunteers to tutor—in her spare time.

If that isn't worthwhile work, what is?

The majority of women who work outside their homes do so not by choice. More than three-fifths of all employed women in this country are single, widowed, divorced, or have husbands who earn less than $7,000 a year. They work because they must.

Those who do choose to be employed feel strongly they

49

are doing what is right—for them. Those who choose to stay home feel they are doing what is right—for them.

Let's hope the day will soon come when neither the woman who is employed nor the woman who works at home will feel defensive about the choices she has made.

We are *all* working women, after all.

But I sometimes forget that fact. Racing to work, racing home for dinner, trying to get a day's housework done in two hours, I've occasionally lost sight of the years I was at home.

Once, after the usual taxing day at work, I arrived home to be confronted by the image of the woman who does stay at home, fulfilling all those roles I no longer had time for.

My son spent the afternoon at a friend's house. When he came home he told me all about his friend's mother. She doesn't work—"You know, because his dad makes a lot of money, I guess."

I swallowed that quietly, making a note to give him the old "women can work for fulfillment as well as for money" lecture at a later date.

Then I heard how his friend's mother is always there when he comes home from school, how she bakes cookies and pies and swims with him several times a week at the YMCA in the middle of the afternoon.

This paragon of motherhood is, in my son's word, "really neat." She doesn't ask her son to help as much around the house, doesn't get tired, is a member of the school cafeteria committee, and a Cub Scout den mother, to boot.

I smiled sweetly through all that, nodding until I felt

like one of those birds that dip into glasses of water, then, later, realized I absolutely loathed this mother—a woman I've never met.

Why? Because I work and she doesn't. It's as simple as that. And from somewhere deep inside came the gnawing guilt again, back to haunt me just when I thought I'd banished it forever.

Most of us who work tell ourselves we wouldn't have it any other way. We believe (most of the time) that our children profit from having working mothers. They're more independent, more able to handle whatever situation may come up. They see women not just as other people's wives and mothers but as individuals with hopes, ambitions and frustrations of their own.

Our daughters may be more assertive than we've been, because they'll have profited from watching us learn to stand on our own two feet and say what we think, no matter what.

And when our sons are grown, they may not have preconceived ideas of where a woman's place is, but may instead allow their wives and daughters to do—and be—whatever is right for them.

Most of us hope and believe all those things will result from our doing—and being—what's right for us. And we know beyond a doubt that the income we earn helps make our families' lives more comfortable.

But, now and then when we least expect it, the old working mother "guilties" creep up and hit us over the head. Sometimes it's a school play we must miss, sometimes a child with the sniffles who stays home alone because we simply can't miss another day on the job.

51

Sometimes we wonder if we're making a big mistake depriving our children of something they need, giving them cause to resent us later because we worked.

I do it. I'm sure you do, too. Then, sooner or later, I run into one of those mothers who stays home and hates it and I realize that's just how I'd be if I gave up what's right for me.

Several days later, my son's friend came over to our house. It was Saturday. He'd been here less than an hour when he wandered into the kitchen and said, "What do you do at work?" I told him, and his eyes were wide. "Wow! That's neat. My mom doesn't do anything," he said.

I could have kissed him.

PART II

Working Wives

9

Husband or Career? Choice Is Not Easy

Which would come first, your husband or your career? The automatic answer to that cliché question is, "My husband, of course."

Which, like most automatic answers, is an easy one—though it may cross a woman's mind that she has never heard a man asked the question, "Which would come first, your wife or your career?"

Mary would have answered that first question automatically. She knew there was a chance her husband, Ken, would be transferred by his company, where he had worked for nine years trying to break into management.

But she had too much on her mind to think about it much. In six years, with no college education, Mary worked her way up from a file clerk position to a management job with a national insurance company.

Then, a year ago, she was selected to participate in an upper echelon management training program that would have assured her of a top position in the company's personnel department in eighteen months.

"I'm ambitious. I know that. I'm willing to work hard for what I want, and that's what I've been doing for the past six years. It's been very satisfying and I love it," she said.

But curled up on a sofa in front of her fireplace, she looked quite defenseless. Perhaps because she is.

Last month her husband told her he had been transferred to another city by his company where there were no branch offices of her insurance company.

"It was what we'd waited for, for nine years. It was the dream come true—Ken finally getting into management," she said, staring into the fire.

"I love him. I know I do. But I've worked so hard to get where I am, and just because I'm a woman, that's not supposed to matter. I'm angry—I never thought I could be this angry, way down inside.

"I always knew he'd be transferred, but not now, when I'm just getting going. Finally—finally, Mary is getting going. Mary is someone, she's someone who has talent and ability and it's the first time, the first . . . ." her voice trailed off.

It did not help one bit that her husband understood. His gentleness and concern only made it worse, made her feel more guilty.

"He's worked too long and hard for this chance. He's my husband and he's a good father, too."

And so, within a week, she had answered the question—her husband would come first.

Mary will work somewhere at something. She has known since her daughter was a year old that she wasn't meant to stay home full time.

This, Mary knows, is the first of what will be many moves in the years ahead. It is expected that people in her husband's new position will move every two years, from city to city.

So it isn't just this job that she's giving up, it's hope for a long-term career with any company.

And the question must be raised, once more. Will you continue to choose your husband over your career—not once but over and over, each time this happens?

The pain was apparent, now—on her face, in her voice. "I don't know," she whispered, "I just don't know. What am I going to do? I can't give up this marriage and I can't be something I'm not—a housewife or a secretary—holding job after job with no challenge."

Perhaps, someday, she will not go with him. And even this time, with the question answered, she knows her answer will have an effect on their marriage.

"But then I suppose I'm human, too. I have needs and I've worked hard to get where I am. We do love each other, and maybe that will be enough—I don't know. I don't have all the answers, not yet anyway," she said.

"Maybe there are no answers," she said.

Perhaps not—but it may be that eliminating cliché questions and automatic answers is a step in the right direction.

Working couples *do* have their own particular problems. But what about the couple in which the wife works and the husband does not? What happens to the traditional male role of provider—and the woman who is breaking untraditional ground?

57

This couple began well. But the end . . . I'm not sure about.

He approved of her job when she had to work. He pitched in, encouraged her, let her know how much he appreciated the effort she was making.

"That was when he was out of a job and we had to have the money," she said. "But about six months after he found another job he announced it was time for me to quit and 'go back to being a wife and mother.' As if I'd ever stopped!

"The problem is, it's too late for that. I've discovered I love working, having my own career. I will not give up—not now. For the first time I feel like I'm somebody, not just somebody's wife and somebody's mother."

She is thirty-five years old, has been married eleven years, and is the mother of a ten-year-old and a seven-year-old. She's also an assistant loan officer for a bank in the Southwest, earns "more than I ever thought I could" and has been promoted twice in a year.

Her husband, an accountant for a large construction firm, for a long time assumed she was happy staying home. She described their marriage as "peaceful. Not very exciting, maybe, but comfortable."

Then, a year ago, her husband lost his job. Part of a "general cutback," he was told.

"He looked for a job for three months. It was horrible. . . ." She paused, searching for words. "He was so . . . demoralized, so upset. I heard there was an opening at the bank and applied, without even telling him," she said.

"When I got the job we had a celebration—went out to

dinner and blew $30, just because we knew money would finally be coming in.

"I got all the support in the world from him, those first four months. Then, he found another position—a better one than he'd had, in fact. And that's when he started talking about my quitting. He was gentle about it at first. But he isn't now," she said.

He says the job has changed her, changed their relationship.

"Of course it has! I'm much more self-confident now. I have a better self-image and it makes me less subservient," she said.

"I do demand of him now, and of the kids too. I ask that they all do their share, no more than that. I am not going to quit a job I love to make a grown man feel secure."

What will happen to her marriage?

"I just don't know. I still love him, I still want to be married to him," she said, shaking her head.

"But I have to be me, first of all. If he doesn't want me the way I am, I suppose our marriage might end. That would make me very sad, and I know it would make our children sad, too.

"But if it happens, I'll have to handle it as best I can. I don't think it will; I think we're going through a difficult time now, but that he'll eventually accept me for what I am—not for what I used to be."

She lit a cigarette, stared at the smoke for a minute, then said softly, "But if he can't, if he wants me to go back instead of forward, I guess neither of us would be happy living together.

"I didn't know this would happen, when I had to go to

work. But it has. I've changed, grown. My horizons have expanded. I cannot—will not—narrow them again.

"And like the song says, I gotta be me. Right now, me is a woman with a career I love and a family I love. I wouldn't let my career force me to give up my family. But I cannot let my family force me to give up my career, either," she said.

"If I did, I'd be living a lie. And that wouldn't be good—for any of us."

Sometimes, there is another side.

John was genuinely pleased when Beth announced she was going back to work; he had encouraged her to do so for some time. She asked if he would share child-care and household responsibilities, and he quickly agreed that was only fair.

She threw herself into her new job with a large insurance agency—free at last (she said) to give herself a career, as John had while she stayed home with two babies.

She asked if he would pick the children up at a day-care center, now and then, when she had to work late. He readily agreed. Soon, he was picking them up every night. Beth couldn't break away from the office until after 6:30 P.M. Ever. So John fixed supper for them, too, or bought them a hamburger on the way home.

Then, Beth began arriving at the office by seven o'clock every morning ("it's the only chance I have to work without interruptions"), which meant she had to leave her house in a Chicago suburb by 6 A.M.

John dressed and fed the children every morning, then

dropped them off at the day-care center on his way to work. He complained. She became very angry. He gave in.

Four months later, Beth said she would have to spend at least half a day at the office every Saturday ("Just for a couple of months or so, to get caught up"). John spent Saturday mornings doing most of the weekly house-cleaning.

He stopped playing golf during that period. "It isn't worth hearing her bitch and moan about it," he said, curtly, when asked why he had given up a sport he'd enjoyed for fifteen years.

One year after she went to work, Beth was promoted to division-manager of the agency.

She was busier than ever. Now there were client dinners, trips out of town, cocktail parties to attend, and always there was more work to be done late at night at the office.

When she was home, Beth was generally tired, tense and moody. If she had had a bad day (and there were many) John and the children learned to keep their distances.

And then one day, two years after she went to work, Beth announced her husband was suing for a divorce— deserting her. With pain and indignation she said he had moved out, claimed he just didn't want to live with her any more.

Beth wore her broken heart fiercely, insisting she *never* intended to marry again. "Husbands! Who needs them?" she said. "No man is ever going to truly accept a wife who has a rewarding career. They're all chauvinistic at heart and you're better off without them anyway."

Which may or may not be true, depending on your point of view. What *is* true is that John and Beth are real people, and that she sacrificed her marriage, children, friends, and her own well-being for the sake of a career.

Beth is by far the exception, rather than the rule. If there are sacrifices to be made, most working women take from themselves first, their careers second, and their families last of all.

But they know what Beth never learned—that with a little thought, with fairness and consideration, they can have both a family and a career. Which is surely the best of both worlds.

Wives who work have often found that however rocky the road, they can succeed with the assistance and comfort of their husbands. But one couple helped me understand just how important a husband's support is. He does *not* support her in her efforts at both a career and a home.

He announced, as he came through the door, that he had a rotten day.

He's tired, fed up with the rat race and seriously thinking of moving into a shack and writing poetry for the rest of his life.

She knows this, too, will pass. Gently, she suggests he take the newspaper into the living room for some peace and quiet. Softly, she asks if he'd prefer to eat late tonight. Carefully, she makes sure the children don't disturb him—at least for a little while.

She's had a rotten day too. Nothing she has done has turned out right. She's exhausted, fed up with being a working woman and seriously wondering if she should give up and stay home.

"Well, you don't have to work, anyway. Why don't you quit? You know I'll take care of you," he says, in his best Papa Bear voice.

Which is just what she did not need to hear—in any voice.

"Why is it that any time I complain, he suggests I quit? I wouldn't think of saying that to him, when he complains. Can you imagine what he'd say if I suggested he quit and let me take care of him? He'd be furious—and rightly," she fumed, at my kitchen table one evening.

"My job is just as important to me as his is to him. But he doesn't seem to understand that."

He was astonished, when presented with that point of view.

"You're kidding! I don't think her job is unimportant at all. I just didn't want her to think she has to work if she doesn't want to. She can quit any time if she wants to, that's all," he said.

His career means more to him than just a weekly paycheck. His self-image, self-confidence and feelings of self-worth depend, to some extent, on his performance at the office.

Her career means more than just a weekly paycheck, too. Her self-image depends on her ability to manage her career and family responsibilities, too.

"I don't dare admit that I've had a bad day. I don't ask for much help around the house, either, because his attitude is that I ought to handle everything, since I *choose* to work," she said.

"He acts as if I've taken up an amusing little hobby—

63

and if it isn't fun all the time I can just quit, walk away."

His attitude may be well-intentioned. Certainly it's not uncommon, a marriage counselor said.

"A husband who reassures his wife by suggesting she quit her job may be reassuring himself, not her. He's asserting over and over that he's perfectly capable of supporting the family.

"He may feel his own, traditional role as provider for the family is being threatened if his wife works. He may fear his wife thinks less of him, or is less dependent on him, because she has her own career," he said.

"To suggest she resign makes it clear he can handle the family's financial burdens—which may involve his own definition of what a man is."

Knowing that may not make it any easier, when a woman feels her job isn't being taken seriously. But if she can see her husband's attitude as a cry for reassurance, rather than a put-down, she may not take it so personally.

"And that," the counselor said, "is certainly going to help."

Yet another couple shows the real pain that can result when husband and wife clash over her work. She works, and expects him to pitch in around the house. He works, and suspects she's forsaken the things they agreed upon when they were married.

She spent years at home while their children were young. Her husband, an advertising executive, worked long hours and the day-to-day care of house and children fell mostly to her.

For the most part, she didn't complain. When she did,

he explained that you have to work long hours to get ahead in the business world.

The children grew and times changed—she works too, now, though she never planned to . . . in the business world, where you still have to work long hours to get ahead. But there's a catch. She says:

"When he was clawing to get ahead, I was home to take care of the children. He could count on that when he was working late three and four nights a week.

"Now that we're both working, I think I should be able to count on him sometimes if I have to work late. But I can't unless it happens to be convenient for him.

"I can't always find a sitter at the last minute, so I've had to say 'no' a couple of times already when the boss has asked me to work a little late. I'm sure not going to get promoted if I keep that up!

"My husband and I could at least take turns, pitching in when the other has to work late—that would be fair. But he won't see it that way."

Then, there is his side of the story:

"Look," he said, stabbing the air with a pencil, "We got married in 1962, when people were doing that kind of thing. She wanted children—she had children. She knew when she had them she would be staying home. We never even discussed her working.

"Yes, I worked hard—still do. I'm the vice president of this agency, I make a good living, I work hard for it. Nothing's changed about that, it's always been true.

"But she's changed. Overnight, she wants to be a working woman—liberated. Fine. Great. But she can't expect

65

me to jeopardize my career because she's decided to have one.

"She doesn't have to work. She wants to. But we've got kids—she knew that when she got the job. Someone has to be responsible for them and it's her responsibility. Period."

She said, her voice low, "I love him, but sometimes I wish I hadn't married him. I never knew how unfair he could be until I went to work."

He said, "Nothing has changed around here, except her. Now she wants the whole world to change because she's working. That's her problem, not mine."

Neither seems to hear what the other is saying.

And *that* may be a problem we all share, at one time or another.

10

"I Had a Problem—
He Didn't"

Susan Fawcett. Successful poet. Feminist.

Formerly a teacher at Bronx Community College, New York, she is co-author of *Grass Roots: The Writer's Workbook* and has published poetry in several national magazines.

Her husband of one year is successful, too. A "liberated" human being, he wants a relationship based on equality rather than stereotypes. He says to her (and others) that it's only right and fair for men to assume half of the household responsibilities if both husband and wife have a career, for example.

In short, it sounds as if Susan Fawcett, 31, has it made. But she has fears, too, and is willing to share them.

She's afraid her husband will tire of a relationship in which he must meet her halfway—which sounds fine in the abstract but boils down to washing the dishes every other night. And doing half of the cooking and half of the laundry.

She fears resentment—his. She's afraid he'll feel

threatened by her career, her success. He says he doesn't, says he's happy for her, content in the relationship.

"But it's still hard to take his word for it. I have friends who say 'Watch out, Susan. Be Careful. You're doing so well, he won't be able to accept it.' And I get terrified, thinking they might be right, I might lose him," she said.

"I used to prod him, back him into a corner with question after question about how he felt. And then, finally, I realized I had a problem—he didn't. I was laying my own fears on him, asking him over and over about his feelings when he'd already *told* me how he felt.

"I had a hard time taking his word for it because I was taught (like most little girls) that men don't express their emotions, that they say one thing and feel another. And I kept right on trying to 'read' him, even though we have a totally different relationship from the one my parents had.

"I try, now, to be very conscious of my own fear, to accept that it exists. And I try to talk openly with him about it. Instead of laying it on him, I lay it on me, where it belongs," she said.

"I just tell him that I'm feeling nervous about being so happy with my work, that I'm afraid it will affect our relationship.

"Then I listen to what he says, try to really hear it and accept it at face value. If he says he's content and happy, I try to accept that—and believe he will also tell me if there is a problem.

"I don't always succeed, but I sure do try. We still have problems—everybody does. But we're getting there," she said.

I don't know anyone who has overcome all the problems. But saying what we feel, instead of beating around the bush, might be a good first step. And accepting what our husbands say, without interpreting and reading our own fears into it, might be a good second one.

Toward the end of our talk, I asked what made her (and the women she knows) truly angry. Was it unequal pay for equal work? Lack of political representation? Inequality in the courts?

No, she said.

"It isn't the big issues that cause anger—it's housework, still! No matter how far we go, we're still faced with it. And no matter what husbands *say,* they still never do enough—never really share the burden."

Surprised, I asked other working women what made them really angry—and many of them agreed with Ms. Fawcett.

"Of course it's housework! He helps out, but it's still my responsibility. He lends a hand, but only if I ask him each time," said an assistant editor at a large, daily newspaper.

Another working wife shook her head when asked about anger. "I can't put my finger on it, really. My husband is generally loving, helpful and supportive.

"But there are no assumptions in his corner. It isn't assumed he will cook, and clean, and do the laundry and make out grocery lists—all the things it is assumed I will do, even though I have a full-time job, too.

"So if he does any of those things, I feel I have to be appreciative for the extra effort. I thank him, when he offers to do the grocery shopping. He doesn't thank me if I do the laundry. It's as simple as that," she said.

69

"And he's the cream of the crop! I know for a fact he's better about sharing home responsibilities than most of the husbands I know. But it still isn't equal, because it's still my responsibility. And responsibility wears you down, after a while."

The message is still clear, said Ms. Fawcett. "If you work, you still have to do everything. If your work doesn't interfere with homemaking, fine. But your first obligation is to the home. The message is definitely loud and clear.

"And the women I know feel such anger over the housework they're still faced with, and the ploys men use to get out of really sharing it.

"Men play the game of not knowing how, of never being able to do anything quite right, and it's insulting to have to go back and back, again and again, and explain and play the childish games," she said.

Finally, a psychologist summed it up. "The whole problem with the women's movement is that they only tell me how things should be—they don't tell me how to cope with the way things are.

"Of course my husband should do more, at home. Of course that makes me very angry, sometimes. But I'm not going to divorce him after nineteen years because he doesn't do the laundry, am I?" she said.

"And I'm not going to give up a career I love, either. So I'm going to keep on doing more than my share, keep on getting angry, and keep on hoping things will change, someday.

"Maybe most of us are doing that—because we just don't have much choice, yet."

11

"We've Chuckled So Long at the Ineptness of Men"

I doubt any working mother spends a full day at the office without thinking about what's going on at home.

"Is the baby catching a cold? He seemed congested this morning. Is Junior really happy staying with a neighbor after school? He seems so brusque when I pick him up after work.

"Susie is so whiny in the morning. Is she just a slow riser, or does she hate that nursery school? And what is Billy really doing after school? Is he content staying home alone, or is he hiding the fact that he's lonely and miserable?"

Like it or not, a mother is still the "psychological parent" in most families—the one who feels ultimately responsible for the physical and emotional well-being of each child.

We are the ones who know how they sleep, who their teachers are, what stages they're going through, what they like for lunch, what their secret fears are, what's going on in their heads.

Our husbands may help, offer support, share our concerns. But it is we who *feel* responsible, nevertheless. And going to work isn't going to change that overnight.

So while our husbands (and the men we work with) concentrate entirely on the job at hand during the day, we are pulled in several directions. Not only do we work hard, we also keep an eye on the clock, listen for the telephone, and worry a lot.

No wonder we're tired at the end of the day!

The paradox is that no matter how tired we are, we find it difficult to really share the responsibility for child-rearing with our husbands. We may be willing for them to "help out" or "pitch in" around the house. We may insist on it. But allowing them to shoulder responsibility, without our help, is another matter altogether.

Not long ago my husband announced he would pick up number-two child after school and buy him a pair of much-needed new shoes.

"Okay. But don't let him talk you into tennis shoes this time of year. And don't forget to allow room for growth. Oh—and please don't treat him to a lot of snacks. You know how he is, he won't eat a bite of dinner. . . ."

I suddenly realized what I had done. Glad for the offer of "help," I had treated him like a teen-aged baby sitter instead of allowing him to assume responsibility for his own child's needs.

If you think back a moment, you may remember doing the same sort of thing. Most of us have.

But we must learn to share parenting responsibilities if we're to carry full-time jobs and bear children, too.

Jean Curtis, in her fine book entitled *Working Mothers*, says:

"The women's movement has encouraged even the most conventional and satisfied women to ask for help with housework. But women don't know how to ask for a *total* sense of responsibility. We've chuckled so long at the ineptness of men where raising children is concerned that we have come to believe that ineptness is a masculine trait."

I hope our daughters will not "chuckle." The price we pay now for having done so is enormous. It places an exhausting double burden on the more than half of us who now work, and deprives fathers of a sense of real involvement with their own children, as well.

Your husband says he'd be glad to handle certain household chores each week. You thank him for the offer, then change the subject.

Your husband says he's going to stop playing golf every Saturday, to spend more time with the children and help you with the housework. You talk him out of it.

Your husband says he wouldn't mind moving if you were transferred to another city. You thank him, but make it clear to your boss that a transfer would be out of the question.

Listen, as the three women involved in the episodes described above tell us why they reacted as they did:

"He offered to help, but he wanted to take over specific jobs (like the laundry and cleaning the bathrooms) and do them every week. It just sounded too cut and dried—like a business contract. I think he would have resented being obligated that way, and it just wasn't worth it," said the first wife.

The woman whose husband offered to stop playing golf

73

every Saturday shrugged and said, "He's played golf with the same guys every week, and he loves it. I know those guys would give him a hard time about his working wife if he dropped out.

"He'd spend more time with the children, but he would be resenting it every minute— and resenting me, too, or my job. I'd rather do all the housework than have him wanting me to quit—and I'd rather the kids saw him happy one day a week than miserable for two days," she said.

Then there's the wife whose husband offered to move if she were transferred to another city. She is a psychiatric social worker, interested in an administrative position. He is an English professor at a state university, not at all interested in management. They have no children.

"Of course I believe him!" she said. "I think he honestly believes he wouldn't mind moving because of my career. But I think he certainly would mind, eventually.

"By the time he told his family, and they shook their heads; by the time three friends kidded him about not wearing the pants in the family; by the time he actually left the job (which he enjoys) and had to start all over again somewhere else—I think he would resent the whole business. And then it would be too late," she said.

"My marriage is too important for me to risk it."

Three women second-guessing their mates, making decisions based *not* on what was said, but on what might be said—or left unsaid—in the future. I've done it. I'll bet you have, too.

We say we want a better world—one in which people

participate in equal partnerships, say what they mean, level with one another; one in which both men and women can be whole individuals.

The first step might be learning to accept it, when it's offered.

Wives must be reeducated, as well as husbands. Women must be willing to give up responsibility, as well as assume it. And if we are overworked at home, it may be because we choose to be.

That was the consensus when fifty women recently met in Boston for an informal luncheon seminar. One participant, a "happily married college professor," expressed it this way:

"I think most reasonable women are married to reasonable men. I personally don't know a single woman who is expected to work all week and then do all the housework. But I know a heck of a lot of women who do.

"I did too, for a while. And I complained like crazy! But I did it anyway, because I was convinced my husband couldn't—or wouldn't. Or that he couldn't do it 'right'—meaning exactly the way I did it," she said.

"Oh, he tried at first. He did all the laundry for a couple of weeks. But every time he did it, I found something wrong. This was wrinkled, or that wasn't quite clean, or something else didn't feel soft. . . .

"After a couple of weeks, he stopped doing the laundry.

"Then, for a while, he did the grocery shopping. Made out the list and everything. Only he never seemed to find the bargains I used to find. The meat was tough, or too fat, or too expensive. The produce wasn't as crisp as it should have been," she said.

"After a while he stopped doing the grocery shopping.

"If he vacuumed a room, I always spotted a dust ball here, or a toy left under the couch, or a dusty corner there. And I always pointed them out.

"Pretty soon, he stopped doing the vacuuming.

"Then came the explosion. And it was a beauty!" she said, rolling her eyes and laughing.

"I had asked him to mop the kitchen floor for me because we were expecting company. He did. But when he was finished waxing it, it didn't shine much.

" 'Did you rinse the floor before you waxed it?' I asked innocently.

" 'No,' " he said.

" 'It would shine, if you had,' I said."

(We were ahead of her, by now. She raised her voice over the laughter.)

"Well, he let me have it—both barrels. 'I am sick and tired of being treated like a child,' he yelled. 'You complain if I don't do my share—but my share is never good enough. And you never hesitate to tell me about it, either.'

" 'If I can't do it to suit you—you do it. I give up,' he said. Then he stormed out of the house—to cool off, I guess," she said.

"I sat in the living room for a long time, alone, after he left. And realized he was absolutely right. I was being terribly unfair to him. And I would have exploded even sooner if the situation had been reversed.

"When he came back, I was ready. I told him how wrong I had been, and how sorry I was. And I vowed to let him do his share *his* way from then on—if it killed me!

"It almost did for a while," she said. "I'd have to leave the room, so I wouldn't ask him why he bought steak instead of hamburger, or used hot water on something I would have washed in cold," she said.

"But I did it.

"We share housework, now. Rather, we each assume responsibility for certain chores. And if he wants to use molasses instead of soap on the kitchen floor, that's fine with me!"

12

"I Thought He Was the Lucky One"

She was the picture of a perfect wife. Or so she thought. The house was spotless and so were the children; buttons were sewn on promptly; meals were varied and nourishing.

Then she went to work.

Now the house is far from spotless, buttons are lost before they're sewn, meals are a catch-as-catch-can proposition, and her husband is often home before she is. And she's glad of it.

"I'm a much better wife—a better person—than I was before I went to work. And our marriage shows it!" she said. "I understand his problems as I never could before. For the first time, we share—really share—our lives with one another.

"For years, I thought he was the lucky one. I resented the daily drudgery of being a housewife; the constant repetition. I envied his 'outside life'; one I pictured as being stimulating and fun.

"I didn't understand when he came home discouraged

and bitter about his job. I didn't understand when he came home exhausted and tense. Now I understand completely, because I'm living it too," she said.

"I've learned that being a good wife means being a partner, understanding where he's coming from. It has nothing to do with how clean the house is, or how elaborate the meals."

She paused, leaned forward, and touched a marble coffee table in her tastefully furnished living room.

"Before, we had an unspoken arrangement. He earned the money; I spent it. I had very little knowledge about our financial situation. He handled it, for the most part. And we had a lot of arguments because I wanted to spend money he wanted to save," she said, shaking her head.

"Now I understand what it's like to feel a little insecure about a job—to wonder what would happen if I lost it, if suddenly we had much less income than we've been used to.

"It makes me much more security-conscious, more inclined to save part of every paycheck rather than run right out and spend it.

"Most of all, it's made me aware of how difficult it is to work full time and have any time or energy left over. I used to be furious if he didn't feel like playing with the children at night. I used to think, 'He's been away from them all day and I haven't. The least he can do is spend time with them when he's home. They're his too, after all.'

"Now, I know how hard it is to give more of yourself when you've worked hard all day. I know it takes real effort to care about *anything* when you're that tired!

79

"Sometimes he complained about the time he spent commuting every day. How could I understand? I'd never spent an hour in bumper-to-bumper traffic on the Long Island Expressway—before my day's work even started. And I'd never spent another hour fighting noise and traffic, day after day, just to get home," she said.

"Now, I have. And I still feel guilty about the times I dismissed his complaints.

"We work as partners now. We talk more because we share many of the same problems. If he's worried about a political situation in the office, I understand. If I'm particularly tired in the evening, he understands. If we have money problems, *we* have them—and work them out together.

"We share more as parents, too," she said.

"He's much more willing to pitch in at night, knowing I've worked as hard as he has all day. And I'm more understanding if he has to work late, or bring work home.

"What time we do have, we spend with the children— together. Neither of us has that much time with them. But the times we have are better than they've ever been," she said.

"Our marriage is, too."

My husband expressed a similar view recently.

"There are a lot of problems involved in both of us working and raising a family. In fact, there are times when it hardly seems worth it. But most of the time, day in and day out, I wouldn't have it any other way," he said.

"We're partners. We share the breadwinning, the housework, we take an equal part in raising our children.

80

If you knew nothing about the business world and I left the children to you, we'd both be lonely, I suspect."

Food for thought . . . a positive side, less easily measured than the day-to-day, petty annoyances and worries working women face.

A friend (also the husband of a working woman) thought a moment, when asked if there were advantages as well as disadvantages, in having a working wife.

"Sure—the kids," he said. "I know them much better than I did before Mary went to work. I just didn't take much part in raising them when she was home all day. That was her job. Mine was making money.

"Now, we share it because we have to. We're not with them all day, so we spend time with them in the evenings, together. I've had long talks with my son I never would have had before Mary went to work. Before, I didn't have time. Now I make time.

His wife nodded. "I think we're much closer than we were when I was a housewife," she said. "We spend a lot of time running, we don't get to see that much of each other, but when we are together we have a lot more to share. And I feel like I'm more interesting; I have more to say."

Finally, there was a seventeen-year-old whose mother has worked since he was three. (He just came over to mow the lawn, but he's used to strange questions.) Are there advantages in having a working mother?

He scratched his head and grinned. "I think there are a lot of advantages. She isn't nagging me all the time over every little thing, you know? Some mothers are after you all day, just because they're always around.

"I think I get treated more like an adult because she

81

works. She knows I've got good sense—because I do."

A thoroughly unscientific survey, and I quit while I was ahead. But working and caring for a family can be as rewarding as it is exhausting. We work for money. But along with the paycheck, we may be collecting hidden benefits.

A closer, more sharing relationship with our husbands, children reared by two parents, instead of one, a feeling that we have something to offer, that we're doing our part—all can come with the job.

And that's not a bad bonus, every week.

13

"We Can't Stop Seeing People Because We Both Work"

"Don't misunderstand me. I think it's fine if Maggie works. But I don't think it's all right for us to turn into a couple of hermits because of her job," he said.

She hunched forward in her chair. "That's fine for him to say, but he isn't willing to make concessions on account of my job. He thinks we should go right on entertaining like we used to—as long as I go right on doing all the work," she said.

They live in a Chicago suburb, in a neighborhood where dinner parties are a standard way of entertaining friends and neighbors.

"I love giving dinners. I'm something of a gourmet and cooking a really fancy meal for six or eight people is great fun, if you have the time and the energy," she said.

"But cooking a fancy dinner isn't fun at all if you've been working all week, the house is a mess, and you have to spend all day Saturday cleaning, shopping, and cooking—then most of Sunday cleaning up again.

"Most of the women who live here don't work. They can spend all week getting ready for a Saturday night dinner party. I could too, before I went back to work.

"Now, I'm so tired by the time the weekend comes, all I want to do is spend a couple of quiet evenings relaxing, maybe go out to a movie, and get to know the kids again. I'd enjoy going out to dinner, too, and being waited on—for a change," she said.

Now, he leaned forward. "I understand all that—it's funny, I used to try to explain that to her when I worked all week and she was home. She wanted to go, go, go on the weekends.

"But there's got to be a happy medium of some kind. We can't just stop seeing people entirely because we both work. And if you don't invite people over you stop getting invited, it's as simple as that. We've already lost contact with several couples we used to enjoy, and I just don't like it," he said.

Maintaining a social life can be a problem for any couple if both parties work all week. What used to be "normal" entertaining may seem too exhausting to be worthwhile.

The trick, for many, is compromise. Keeping it small and simple.

Instead of giving lavish dinner parties, many working couples simply invite friends over for dessert and coffee or after-dinner drinks. They meet friends for dinner at a favorite restaurant, or invite just a few for Sunday brunch, or Saturday morning coffee and pastry, or to watch a football game on television.

"I was a little self-conscious at first, because I had always entertained with a capital E," said a seasoned working wife.

"But I found that the people we really enjoyed didn't care a hoot whether I served a five-course dinner or potato chips and dip. They came because they liked our company, and they seemed to understand perfectly that I simply didn't have much time, any more.

"Given a choice, I'd rather entertain informally than never entertain at all—and if you work full time, that's just about what it comes down to. You either compromise a bit, or you turn into a recluse. You'll find your real friends will understand. And you don't need to see the others, anyway."

That's one couple's solution to the problem of scheduling mutually enjoyable leisure time. But what about "leisure" time that is actually "company" time—when each works at a job that requires socializing outside the office? Does each have to enjoy the other's coworkers, gatherings and parties?

"I went to his company parties for years. They bored me to death, but I went.

"The people I work with threw a party last weekend and my husband agreed to go; but he was an absolute toad all evening. He said he was bored, he didn't have anyone to talk to, he got tired of hearing shop-talk.

"As if I hadn't suffered through all that at his parties! We had an awful fight, and I'm still furious about it."

Most of us have attended parties as the wife or date of a company man. Generally, men cluster together to discuss golf, business, women and more business while women cluster in a corner to discuss recipes and tips on rearing children.

85

It may bore us to death, but there is seldom a question as to what is expected of us.

Not so for the husband or date of a company woman. We haven't been around long, after all. And it isn't uncommon for males to balk when it comes to attending *her* company party.

"First of all, he doesn't know anyone at the party but me. And while the guys in the office joke and talk with me, he stands around looking awkward and forlorn," one woman said.

"He doesn't fit in with the males because they're my coworkers and we're laughing at inside jokes and talking shop, to some extent, and he doesn't fit in with my coworkers' wives, either."

Another working wife thought the problem went deeper than that, though she said she had been able to overcome it.

"I think at first he had a real hard time dealing with being Barbara's husband at a party. After all, he hadn't had the practice wives have had!

"But for the first four or five parties we went to, I made a concentrated effort to make him feel comfortable. I brought him into conversations and made sure he met men who shared his interests," she said.

"Instead of treating him like a husband, I pretended he was a close friend from out of town attending the party with us.

"It took some extra effort, but before long there were three or four people he looked forward to seeing at every party. And it was more than worth it—because now we both have a good time," she said.

Still another working wife said she and her husband had "finally" solved the whole company problem.

"We don't go. I hated going to his, for years. Now that I work, he hates going to mine. But he thinks he should attend his, and mine give me a rare chance to see the men I work with in a social setting.

"So he goes to his and I go to mine—alone," she said.

"Why should we inflict company parties on each other? I tell the people at my office that my husband doesn't like parties. He tells his office the same about me. Our co-workers may think we're a little weird, but who cares?

"We enjoy our own company parties—and it's one less thing to fight about!"

PART III

On the Job

14

You Can Make the Necessary First Step

You're forty years old and haven't been employed for twenty years. Now you must find a job—quickly! What do you do?

"You panic, if you're like me," Michele said. "I had been a secretary for one year before I married at the age of twenty. Then, two days after my fortieth birthday, my husband and I separated. I had to find a job right away—I needed the income."

She made the rounds, day after day.

"I never even got as far as an interview, and no wonder. The application forms were a nightmare! Previous experience? Twenty years ago. Last place of employment? A company that no longer existed. College degrees? None. Skills? I'd forgotten what little I had known.

"And then one day (when I was on the verge of slitting my own throat) I saw a public service announcement for the YWCA. And that got me to thinking. I had done volunteer work there, and enjoyed it a lot. In fact, I'd organized a girls' basketball team for the kids, and a swimming program, too," she said.

"So I called the area director and asked for an appointment. And she remembered me! I went to see her the next day.

"She said the winter athletic program was floundering, that they had been considering hiring someone to work in a liaison position with the schools—finding girls who would benefit from after-school activities and arranging transportation for them.

"I told her I thought I could handle the job and we talked quite a while. But I left wondering if I'd ever hear from her again. And I didn't, for the longest two weeks of my life.

"But she did call, and she offered me the job—said she had bent some rules, but that she thought I was perfect for it. She said the salary would be low, but when she named the figure I was ecstatic.

"It was enough to get by on, and, besides, I knew I'd love the job. I accepted on the spot," Michele said.

A year later she began attending evening classes at a community college, graduating last June with a four-year degree in physical education.

"I'm not with the YWCA anymore. I work within the school system now, planning athletic programs and after-school activities for high-school girls. I love my job, I'm self-sufficient, and my self-confidence has increased about 100 percent. I guess I'm one of the lucky ones," she said.

Moral? Whether you're twenty, forty, or fifty-five years old there is probably a skill, a natural ability you have which you can utilize in the job market.

You may not have a degree or hard business experience.

But raising children, managing household finances, doing volunteer work in the community all require specific skills which some organization, somewhere in your area, may need.

If you work well with children, why not check the child-care organizations in your town? If you're an avid reader, or good at organization, why not check with local libraries? If you work well with older people, or with those who are ill, local hospitals, nursing homes, and funded centers for the elderly may have a real need for your specific skills.

You may have to start on a part-time basis or at a relatively low salary. But it's a start, a first step. And for most of us, the first step is the hardest one of all.

And then comes the job interview. If you're working you've already had at least one. Chances are you'll have several more before your career is over.

"It doesn't matter how impressive your credentials are; if you can't come across well during a job interview, you're probably going to miss a lot of good opportunities in the job market," said a personnel director for a large insurance company.

She's hired more than one hundred women during the past year. And, she said, we seem to have an especially difficult time with interviews.

"You've got to sell yourself during an interview. Being shy or modest isn't going to accomplish anything. You've got to project self-confidence, seem assured and positive. But a lot of women seem unable to do that," she said.

"At some point during the conversation you're bound to be asked what your qualifications are for a particular job. If you look down, stutter, stammer and mumble—what is the interviewer supposed to think?"

She shook her head. "Practice at home—out loud—if you have to. But before you ever make an appointment for a job interview, you ought to have a clear idea of what job you're applying for and an extremely clear idea of what your qualifications are," she said.

Then there's the matter of listening. Most people (men and women) don't do enough of it before they answer those questions the interviewer throws from behind the desk.

"Pay attention to what's being said. Think. If you're asked a question that isn't clear to you, ask for clarification before you try to answer it.

"Too many people think they'll seem dense if they do that. What they don't realize is that they seem a lot denser if they spend ten minutes not answering the question that was asked," the personnel director (who admitted she, too, had "blown" a few interviews in the past) said.

The ideal interview is a mutual exchange of information, she added. It's a way to find out about the company, while the company finds out about us.

"Too many people see it as a win-lose situation. They either get the job or they don't, they're accepted or they're not. But a job interview is simply a way of determining if they would be right for a particular job, and if it would be right for them.

"Remember, most companies are just as interested in the person who is being interviewed as he or she is in the ccmpany. We want good people, every company wants good, promotable people. We may be as eager as you are—it just doesn't show so much," she said.

Finally, you may do all the "right" things and still not get the job.

"But that doesn't mean you've wasted your time, unless you see it that way. Every job interview can be a learning experience if we just use it as such," she said.

"Each time we answer a question about ourselves, we learn something about ourselves. Each time we see a new company up close, we learn something about companies in general. And each time we get through a job interview, we've probably learned how to do a better one next time."

A good way to prepare for your interview is to ask yourself some of the questions you're sure to be asked during the next job interview. The answers can tell you a lot about where you want to go.

"Where do you want to be in five years?" A typical job interview question, and a tough one for many of us. We're just learning to set concrete goals for ourselves in relation to our careers. But if you're entering the labor market, or changing jobs, it's a crucial one.

"Which is more important to you—your salary, or the work you do?" If you're working because you must, your salary (and its rate of increase) has to be your first consideration. You'll head for a nontraditional job or to companies that pay well in your area; even if working for them is not your idea of heaven.

If you're working because you choose to, on the other hand, you might be willing to earn less for the sheer joy of doing what you want to do.

95

The answer to that one may also help you decide if you'd be willing to go to school or spend six months as a trainee for a particular job—another common interview question.

"How well do you work under pressure?" Some people enjoy daily deadlines, demanding clients, a hectic work schedule. If you do, try not to settle for a routine job. You'll be bored, miserable and looking for another one, soon.

If pressure makes your insides churn, on the other hand, steer clear of jobs which dish it out on a regular basis. There's nothing wrong with disliking pressure—the trick is to know you do before you're caught in it.

"Are you willing to travel?" As women move into management and nontraditional jobs, more of us are being asked to travel. Would you enjoy that? Can you manage it? How much would you be willing to do?

"How flexible is your schedule?" Often, that's another way of asking, "Can you work late?" If you have young children at home, or a demanding husband, or you're a single parent, or you just don't want to work more than a prescribed number of hours a week, you'll look for a position that won't require you to work overtime.

The U.S. Department of Labor's Occupational Handbook lists 1,000 jobs; all, by law, are open to women. Your nearest state employment office offers free aptitude testing, counseling and job-referral services.

"Publications of the Women's Bureau" lists career publications for women. It is available free from the Women's Bureau, Employment Standards Administration, U.S. Department of Labor, Washington, D. C. 20210

Also free is a list of 152 pamphlets devoted to specific

careers, available by writing to Herbert Bienstock, Regional Commissioner, U.S. Department of Labor, Bureau of Labor Statistics, Room 3425, 1515 Broadway, New York, N. Y. 10036.

There is help available if you're trying to choose the career that's right for you. And answering job-interview questions before they're asked can help too.

Rather than look for a job, many women opt for the education they never finished. For reasons as varied as curiosity or a desire to have an educational base upon which to build a career, thousands of women are returning to high school, junior college and college.

But it's not easy, if you're thirty-five, and have been home full time for ten years. In fact, it can be frightening to consider the alien world of school, which is now populated by others much younger and better prepared.

The first thing to remember is that you're not alone, said Dr. Bernice Sandler, director of the Project on the Status and Education of Women for the Association of American Colleges, located in Washington, D. C.

"Women who have been home with families are going back to work in increasing numbers. They're going back earlier than used to be the case (before their children are grown) and, generally, it's due to economic necessity," she said.

"They're divorced, or widowed, or have simply found that raising children becomes a more expensive proposition as the children grow older. Orthodontists, college and clothing expenses and a higher standard of living have all made it necessary for women to be wage-earners, too."

97

Which, for many of us, means brushing up on old skills, taking a course or two, or earning a high school or college diploma in order to get a better job.

Dr. Sandler suggested collecting all the information on adult education in your community before making a final decision about going back to school.

"The library is an excellent place to start—perhaps the best. Library bulletin boards often contain all sorts of information on adult education, counseling centers and other community resources for women," she said.

Next, check with local YWCA offices, your school board and all the universities, colleges and community colleges in your area to find out what adult education programs are available.

If you live in a metropolitan area, there may be counseling centers nearby, geared to help women who are trying to reenter the labor market. These can be very helpful if they are attuned to women's problems, Dr. Sandler said.

"The counselors must know what it's like to be forty-five, widowed, and untrained for a job that pays decently. Or they must know what it's like to be thirty, to have to go to work to support a family and not have a high school diploma," she said.

Finally, it might help your self-confidence to know you have a good chance of succeeding, if you do decide to go back to school.

"Women who go back tend to be highly motivated, get better grades and stay longer than first-time students.

"They come into the classroom with definite goals in mind, or develop goals very quickly. They don't flounder as long as first-time students, they have enough maturity to buckle down and get the job done," Dr. Sandler said.

"Going back to school at any age can be a frightening prospect; but more and more women are doing it. It's a well-traveled path, though sometimes you may feel you're the only one on it."

15

Maybe Men Will Begin to Imitate Us!

It probably would be wise to tell you, before you read any further, that this is guaranteed to make most working women furious.

It's going to do what most of us have been trying *not* to do for a number of years—point out the differences between working women and working men.

I can't report on the attitudes of all men, but I can tell you what two separate interviews, one with two men and one with three, revealed about how those men felt, deep down, about working women.

The five men I talked with were executives, under the age of forty, educated and articulate. All had women working for them. Three also worked with women on a peer level.

All of them asked not to be identified because, as one put it, "Every woman in the office would quit—and that would be the least that could happen. Probably I'd end up in court and out of my own job, to boot."

"Women's lib has gotten us to the point where we can't

treat women equally. We have to treat them with kid gloves.

"I have the feeling if I want to let a woman go—fire her—I'd better get a lawyer first to be sure I'm not going to get hauled into court," a bank executive said.

There are some characteristics "most" working women exhibit that drive these five men up the wall, they said.

We're too emotional, we don't solve our own problems, won't make decisions fast enough; we bring our personal lives into the office, and we take everything much too personally—pout, sulk and have hurt feelings for days over something that a man would have forgotten in ten minutes.

"You wouldn't see a man coming into the office the day after he'd had a fight with his wife and telling five people that he's tired because of this fight he had and how his wife doesn't understand him, and on and on.

"But you sure would know it if a girl broke up with her boyfriend or a woman's kids were sick. A lot of times I know more than I want to know about my female employees' lives," said the bank executive.

Would they be comfortable working for a woman? The answer from all of them was a resounding *no*. No concrete answers about why they feel that way, just vague expressions of uneasiness.

"I'll tell you one thing, though. In some ways it's easier to handle a woman who's on the same level—like a client.

"A woman will back down where a man wouldn't take it. I'll just say, 'Sorry, it can't be done that way' to a woman, and I wouldn't dare say that to a man," one of the advertising executives said.

101

And if she doesn't back down? "That really burns me up. It really rips me to have a woman do that," the man admitted, then grinned sheepishly.

Finally, who's the least welcome candidate for a job opening? These men said divorcees with young children would be first on the list. "Too many problems, too unstable," were a few of their main reasons.

The points these men made aren't true of all women, they said, but, as one said, "They're true often enough so I'm definitely aware of them. A lot of women are completely professional all the time—I admire them. But a lot aren't; that's all there is to it."

So, now we know some of the impressions we may be fighting. It helps, I think, to know what we're up against—even if it's unfair, even if it makes us angry.

And if we're just a little bit guilty of anything these five men said, maybe we can begin changing now.

A letter from a woman in Canada summed up "the other side" so well, I thought I'd share part of it with you.

Had five women been interviewed about male characteristics that drive *us* up the wall, their response might have gone something like this, she said:

"Men are too secretive about their emotions. They think they can solve every problem by themselves, make rash and unwise decisions—then defend them to the death, even after they realize they've made a mistake.

"Men bring their personal lives into the office, too, but bottle up their true feelings. The result is that they scream and bitch about everything except what's really bothering them—chew out and bully subordinates for days over something a woman would have gotten off her chest in ten minutes.

102

"You wouldn't see a woman coming into the office the day after she'd had a fight with her husband and telling five people their filing system stinks and their new computer program (yesterday labeled 'brilliant') is inadequate and she's tired of getting her own coffee and heads are going to roll if someone doesn't snap to it and find the erasers!

"And you wouldn't see a woman come into the office after spending the night with one of the mailboys, brag about it to her colleagues, then serenely recommend a raise for the entire mailroom staff.

"But you sure would know it if a guy broke up with his girlfriend, because he'd be making his employees' lives miserable. A lot of times I gain more insight than I care to into my male employees' lives.

"Admittedly, I didn't conduct any interviews and my female executives are purely hypothetical. The point to be made here is, simply, that there are two sides to every coin," this woman said.

She's right, of course. And some of the accusations leveled by those five men seemed unjustified and unfair—generalizations usually are.

But a man's preconceived notions about working women can affect our chances of success before we ever interview for a job in his office, or his department. Whether what he thinks is true or untrue, it's going to affect his attitude toward us.

If we're aware of what his feelings might be (if we know what we're up against) we're that much ahead before we start.

I would never suggest we try to imitate the men in our offices. We've watched male executives alienate their

103

families, develop ulcers and have early heart attacks, all in the name of "getting ahead." Why would we want that?

Instead, perhaps we can learn from each other. If women are comfortable in competitive situations and men are at ease with their own emotions, it can't help but be a better world—for both of us.

Not all men in management view women as do the five we just saw. But there are enough like them to warrant caution, especially if you work for a man.

Remarkably, women who work for women reveal feelings which are just as strong with regard to their bosses.

They are either the best or the worst. They are warm, sympathetic and positive. Or they are cold, demanding and difficult. They're either on our side, or out to get us.

They are women; they are bosses. And whatever else might be true of them, one thing is sure—they evoke strong emotions, one way or the other, from their employees.

"I'd rather work for a woman any time. I've had a woman boss in the past and I have one now. I think women understand better than men what motivates people, said a secretary in the personnel department of a large credit company.

"Men tend to bark and order and expect you to obey without question. A woman will take time to explain what she wants—and she'll tell you when you've done a good job, not just when you've made a mistake."

Another secretary said, "A woman boss understands what it's like to be a working woman. My boss knows I have to have some warning if I'm going to work late, for example. A male boss will throw a stack of letters on my desk at five o'clock, and ask me to work late for no good reason, then get annoyed if I mention I have small children alone at home.

"How can a man understand my problems? Most of them have wives at home to worry about details like hungry children. I'd much rather work for a woman," she said.

A department store buyer who has worked for both men and women said, "The men I've had as bosses have been terribly concerned about work-flow and profit margins. But they didn't care at all about their employees as people.

"For them, I did what I had to. But the two women I've worked for have been marvelous. They made it clear they cared—about people, not just machinelike performance. I think women have a way of bringing out the best in people—in and out of the office. For them, I worked my head off," she said.

Negative reactions to women as bosses?

"I'll never work for a woman again—never!" said an administrative assistant. "Once was enough. I never knew what kind of day I would have because it all depended on her mood. Some days she'd be jolly and easy to work for, other days she'd be an absolute witch. Unprofessional, you might say. You wouldn't see that in a man—or I never have."

And the men she has worked for have been more open, said a former newspaper reporter. "I've worked for two women editors and I never knew what they were thinking! They'd talk about me behind my back, when I couldn't defend myself. But to my face? Never.

"Men will level with you, tell you what they're thinking and clear the air. Women bosses are sweet to your face, then take it out on you behind your back," she said.

Furthermore, said a city employee, women who have made it into management aren't always so eager to help another working woman.

"You would think a woman who'd made it would want other women to, too. Ha! I've worked for two, and both were scared to death of every other woman around. No one could please them, because doing a good job meant you were a potential threat," she said.

"It shouldn't be that way, but it sure was. . . ."

Some women bosses are surely as praiseworthy as those described here. And some are as guilty. But most, I suspect, fall somewhere in between.

Women do have a tough time in management—not because of their own performances, but because of other people's expectations.

That's what several managers said recently, when asked to comment on the problems women face as bosses.

"First of all, there aren't many of us, yet. We have so few role models to follow. We're still something of an oddity. We're watched more closely, judged more harshly. And we are combating factors male executives never think about," said an insurance agency supervisor.

"I am the first woman to go into middle management here. I am responsible for twenty-three people—eighteen women and five men. I've been here a year, and so far I feel quite comfortable with the people I supervise.

"But the first three months in this job were absolute hell. I felt all kinds of resentment from people higher up. It was really thick for a while," she said.

Why?

"I don't know. But I do know that when I took over this job I was told absolutely nothing—I had to find out everything for myself, learn everything the hard way.

"I felt as if they promoted me, then sat back and waited for me to fail," she said.

"They resented me (and still do) because I represented a real threat, I suppose. I've come this far, and what's the next logical step for me? It is to take one of their jobs, naturally. I'm competing directly with them now, and they're scared to death.

"Furthermore, they see the deck stacked against them because I'm a woman and women are being promoted in large numbers in this company now."

But another employer said resentment comes not from her own bosses, but from the seven people (five of them men) she supervises.

"I was the first woman to go into management here. I was, in other words, the first woman to be in a hiring-firing position of authority. And there are still times when I can't win, after two years," she said.

"If I'm objective and businesslike, they see me as a castrating female. But if I'm warm and concerned about them on a personal level, they see me as a pushover—and they're quick to take advantage.

"So I constantly tread this fine line between being too hard and too soft. I can't just be me—do what comes

107

naturally. I'm never viewed as just another boss; I'm viewed as a woman boss, or a woman who happens to be a boss," she said.

"People accept male authority figures—father figures. But a mother figure? They're just not supposed to be in positions of authority, in most people's minds."

Still another employer, who supervises nineteen women in a large hospital's business office, agreed. But, she said, the situation is improving—slowly.

"Of course women are still judged by different standards. The expectations people have about bosses in general is that they will be objective, fair, professional, forthright, tough sometimes and in control of the situation at all times," she said.

"And people haven't changed their expectations of women as much as we like to think. We're still supposed to be warm, maternal, compassionate, people-oriented, soft and easily manipulated.

"So what happens? If we live up to what people expect of bosses, we lose—because we've failed as women. If we fulfill their expectations about women, we lose—because we're ineffectual managers.

"I think we can be both. A good boss *is* warm, compassionate, and people-oriented. A good boss is also objective, professional and can be tough if that's required. And a woman can be all those things and still very much a woman," she said.

"I know that—you know that. Pretty soon everyone will know that. The day will come when we'll just be bosses—good or bad, not male or female. It isn't here yet, but it will be."

Once you're in a high-level position, one of your primary concerns is your relationship with the men at your level. As a woman, are you treated fairly, with an equal share of the work, responsibilities and rewards? And, more importantly, are you allowed to participate in the events and decisions affecting your business?

A constant point of contention among women I talk to is that they are all too often isolated. They just are not included in what they should be included in. A good instance of this is the exclusion of women from an important—if unofficial—aspect of any office.

Tom applied for a better job with a competing company because he "heard" there was an opening coming up. He got the job.

Bill is staying right where he is. He's "heard" a vice-president will retire soon, and he's next in line.

Call it gossip, office politics, company intrigue—the fact is a great deal of useful information is exchanged in the men's room, locker room, on the golf course and at the corner bar.

Women are excluded from most of it.

And, as one executive said, "It's important to know what's going on in a company—which way the wind is blowing. Anyone who thinks she can rise above it all just isn't being realistic. And reading the monthly newsletter isn't going to tell you what you need to know."

When she was promoted to a management position she found herself "in a cocoon," she said.

"Like a lot of women today, I was the only female executive in the company. I felt totally isolated. The guys got together after work and planned golf games and ten-

nis matches for the weekends. I wasn't one of them because I'm a woman.

"And once I was promoted, the women I had worked
with seemed uncomfortable around me. Suddenly I was
management and not to be trusted," she said.

Solutions? There's no way to barge into the men's room
or insist on being included in the next golf game. But you
can cut down on the isolation *if* you take the initiative,
and *if* you help the men see you as just another coworker,
seasoned career women say.

"You have to overcome your own shyness first, and you
have to be willing to endure some uncomfortable moments. But remember, they don't know how to handle
you, either. They're not used to working with women as
equals—too few of us have made it to management," said
one.

"When the guys head for lunch in a cluster, leaving you
behind, grab your purse and go with them—even though
you haven't a formal invitation.

"There may be some long silences the first time or two.
But after a while you'll be accepted and included; especially if you don't emphasize the fact that you're female,"
another said.

"If your attitude is casual and confident, theirs will be
too. Pretty soon, they won't think anything of it—and
you'd be amazed how much you can learn over a tunafish
sandwich," she said, "without asking a single question!"

The same technique can work when the "gang" (male)
heads for the corner bar after work.

"Just ask if you can join them. What are they going to
say? And remember, it's important," said a bank personnel manager.

110

"Then be sure to do three things: have one or two drinks—no more; insist (quietly) on paying for your own; and leave with the group at least the first time or two, which precludes any misinterpretations about your motives, moral character, etc.

"Oh, and relax and have a good time! If you're fun to be with, they'll want you along. Being the first woman in management is never easy; it's not only important to feel comfortable with the men—it's a lot less lonely," she said.

"I'm going to make it, though. And I think a lot of women will be joining me before too long."

Another frequent complaint from women is the double standard applied to the emotional responses of men and women.

If a man pounds the desk or slams a door, he's being forceful. If a woman raises her voice or slams a door, she's being a bitch. Or so the saying goes.

So how does a woman handle occasional anger in a business situation without jeopardizing her career?

Dr. Jane Norton, manager in the Finance and Data Processing Unit of Boston University (the only female supervisor in the department), thinks we need not imitate men in learning how to express anger.

"We really don't have role models yet, because there are so few women in executive positions. We haven't been educated for the roles we're facing today," she said.

"But if we try to be men in the office, we will only be poor copies of a man.

"There are alternatives to anger—and they're generally more effective anyway. Sometimes it's best to walk away

111

from a confrontation and cool off; then use intuition, observation, experimentation and positive manipulation, instead of anger.

"It's so important to keep your dignity, to stay feminine and courteous. There is no need to swear, for example, just because a man does. You can tell someone off beautifully just using the English language," she said.

"Intuition is invaluable in assessing a situation. And women can use this traditionally female tool to good advantage. It can help you decide which approach to use with a particular individual.

"Observation is important, too. Seeing the situation as it really is, making sure you're being as objective as possible, often eliminates the need for anger."

Experimentation is a bit more difficult, Dr. Norton admitted. It involves making mistakes now and then, and being willing to change.

"But don't be afraid to make mistakes. See what goes and what doesn't go. One approach might work beautifully on two people and not at all on the third. It makes more sense to experiment than to get angry," she said.

"If you're flexible, intuitive and willing to experiment you'll seldom have a reason to be angry."

The word "manipulation" produces negative feelings in many of us. But Dr. Norton believes positive manipulation is a good alternative to anger.

"Positive manipulation simply means showing your commitment to the job and genuine interest in the people around you. Women have traditionally been the socializers, anyway. We're the ones who keep in touch with families, call neighbors occasionally, keep the party go-ing," she said.

"And there's nothing wrong with that! It's an ability that reflects our interest in people—and that can be a useful tool in the male-oriented business world."

"Anger often results from a lack of awareness, a lack of understanding, or our own insecurities," Dr. Norton added.

"So it's always helpful to pinpoint exactly what it is that's making you angry. What is causing it exactly? If you know that, you can decide on an alternative, instead of building yourself into a box—which is what anger does. Blowing up seldom accomplishes anything," she said.

"Traditionally, women have been allowed to express emotion—to cry, become angry or upset. Men have not been allowed that. So we must be careful. If we use anger sparingly, it will be much more effective.

"If we give ourselves time to cool off, learn to think instead of just reacting, we'll find alternatives that are much more effective than swearing or pounding a desk," she said.

"Then, maybe, men will begin to imitate us!"

16

We've Got to Learn the Rules

Put away your pantsuits, slacks, frilly dresses, very high heels and heavy make-up.

That's what twelve executives (six male, six female) had to say when asked if a woman's "image" might keep her from moving to the executive suite.

Well-tailored, conservative clothing—suits, blazers, dresses, tunics and jumpers—are acceptable. Pantsuits are definitely not if you want to look professional, they said.

And they are not alone.

In a recent survey, five hundred executives (men and women) were asked if a woman in a pantsuit would look as if she belonged in their executive offices. More than 400 said no.

In a separate study, people were shown photographs of the same woman wearing two versions of the same suit—one with pants, the other with a skirt.

When asked which "twin" had a better job, a better education, and earned more, 94 percent of the male executives chose the woman in the skirted suit, as did 88 percent of the women.

"Everyone wants to think who they are is important, not how they dress. But, unfortunately, you have to look like a professional if you want to be treated like one—whether you're a man or a woman," said a publishing executive.

"There are signals people pick up without even being aware of it. They do form an impression, based on how you look. And in this competitive job market, why take a chance you won't be taken seriously?" she said.

Recently, Washington consultant Joan Silberman applied for thirty-three different jobs, dressed in pre-selected outfits. When dressed "professionally" she was offered a job in every case but one. When dressed "unprofessionally" she was not offered a single job.

And the experts say colors are important, as well as style. Studies show the darker the clothing, the more authority it projects.

Grays, blues, blacks and pinstripes might help you land a job in a law firm, for example. And warm colors (reds, oranges, browns and greens) could help you establish rapport with the public; they encourage communication.

What should we wear with an outfit? Very little, the executives said.

"If someone applies for a job wearing tons of make-up and a lot of jangling jewelry—or teeters in on five-inch heels—I find it hard to take her seriously," said one.

"She comes across as being frivolous, rather than effective."

One safe way of deciding what to wear is to notice what others wear in your office.

115

"But don't look at the woman next to you. Look at the women who have been promoted; the ones who hold positions you'd like to hold someday," an insurance executive said.

"I stopped wearing slacks and pantsuits two years ago when I noticed the only woman who had been rapidly promoted, here, *never* wore them.

"Now, I have her old job and she's moved even farther up. I can't say my personal dress code had anything to do with that; but it certainly couldn't have hurt," she said.

You and I may think any "dress code" is reactionary, unimportant and insulting. If we move into management positions, we may hope to change the rules of the game—placing all emphasis on a person's ability, rather than his or her appearance.

But unless we know the rules, we may never get into the game.

Once you're into the game, one of your best allies can be candor. Don't *ever* assume your boss knows what's on your mind. He's busy, too, and may not be adept at mind-reading.

For example, there's an opening coming up in the department you've been eyeing for more than a year.

You know about it; five other people in the office do, too. You want it—badly. You think you're qualified, you know given a little time you could do a fine job, and it would be good for your career as well.

So (if you're like many of us) you buckle down and work harder than ever. Lunch hours, coffee breaks and 5:00 P.M. mean nothing to you as you slave away, proving to the boss that you're the one for the job.

Then one day you hear the news. Joe is moving into the new position. How? Why? He hasn't been with the company as long as you, you can run rings around him, he's not *half* as competent, you sputter to yourself.

It could be that while you were being polite and quiet, Joe was in the boss's office explaining why he wanted the job, why he thought he was qualified to assume more responsibility, and how such a move would affect his long-range career goals with the company.

The employer who chose Joe over you may have had no idea that you wanted more responsibility, or that you had career goals of any kind. He may have assumed you were perfectly happy where you were, in fact, since you never indicated otherwise.

Most of us find it extremely difficult to ask for a raise, a promotion, or an advantageous move within a company. We were reared to believe that if nice girls worked hard and demanded little, they would be rewarded—with a husband, a job, children, or whatever else they might desire.

Girls were never taught to be assertive, to demand what was rightfully theirs, because that was "unladylike" and a strike against them right from the start.

We pay for that, still.

Suppose that instead of working like a diligent mouse, *you* had asked for an appointment with the boss? Suppose you had said something along the lines of "Mr. Jones, I understand there is an opening coming up in the such and such department. I feel I'm qualified to fill the spot, and I'd like to tell you why"?

You then could have listed what you think are your

117

strong points—previous experience in that area, related experience in other areas, your willingness to work long hours, any past projects you handled successfully, and so forth.

Finally, you might have mentioned that moving to a new department would fit in well with your own career goals.

Pushy? Too aggressive? Most of us squirm at the very idea of saying such things to anyone, especially the boss.

But unless we let him know we want the job, that we have specific qualifications for the position, and that we think in terms of a long-range career, rather than just a weekly paycheck, it may not occur to him to consider us for the spot.

In the long run, we have nothing to lose by trying. If we're still denied the move or promotion we know at least that the boss had all available information at hand when he made the decision.

And if we sit quietly in the corner we may never be noticed—let alone promoted.

Here's another instance that convinced me candor pays off.

When she went back to work, Kathy and her husband agreed to share most household and child-rearing responsibilities on a fifty-fifty basis.

With two sons, six and seven years old, and a large house in the suburbs there was a lot to be done each evening when her husband came home from his job as a corporate accountant and she finished her day's work as a corporate advertising assistant.

118

"But we pitched in and got it done, and the boys got plenty of attention. If he worked late, I took over. If I worked late, he handled things at home. It worked well, or I guess I just thought it did," she said, shaking her head.

"Then, he dropped the bomb."

The "bomb" was the announcement that her husband wanted a divorce, that he was in love with someone else and wanted his freedom—right away.

"I honestly don't remember much about the next four months. I went through the motions all day until the kids were in bed, then I paced around the house crying half the night, then got up the next day and went through the motions again," she said quietly.

"I couldn't tell anyone, especially at the office, because I was so ashamed and afraid. I guess a lot of people knew something surely was wrong, but I couldn't bring myself to discuss it.

"The boys were frightfully upset and they clung to me out of insecurity, I guess. I couldn't leave them for a minute at night. I was so exhausted after doing everything around the house alone—taking care of the kids, staying awake half the night and working all day—I hardly knew what I was doing," she said.

"I felt like a zombie, and I guess I looked like one, too.

"My job just was unmanageable. I couldn't work late because there was no one at home to pinch-hit for me but I didn't tell my boss the truth, just made up lame excuse after lame excuse and let him think what he wanted," she said.

What he thought was that Kathy, who had been a

119

hard-working, dedicated employee, had turned into a sloppy, irresponsible one. And he called her in, one day, and told her so.

"I cried—just couldn't stop once I got started. I told him what had happened, told him I just couldn't handle the job any more, and offered to quit right away," she said.

"And he was marvelous! He suggested I talk to the company's psychologist if I ever needed to talk and assured me the conversations would be kept strictly confidential. Then he said he thought we could rearrange my work load so I could bring some home in the evening, if necessary.

"Most of all he said, 'You're a good employee, Kathy, much too good for us to lose. Give yourself a little time to adjust, and we'll do all we can at this end.' I thought I had died and gone to heaven, I was so relieved!

"I was never one to bring personal problems to the office. But I'll tell you, if things are getting out of control and you're already doing the best you can, what have you got to lose?" she said.

"Sometimes it's better to level with the people you work for. It may not help, you may lose your job anyway. But unless you give the boss a chance, how is he going to understand, let alone offer help?

"If you're ever where I was, you haven't got a thing to lose by trying honesty. Bosses are people, too. I found that out. It saved my job and maybe my sanity, as well."

Of course, we've got to be able to accept candor, as well—especially when it means criticism.

The boss calls a male employee into his office.

"These plans just aren't going to work, Bob. I think you

120

have some good ideas, but they don't come together. Let's try it again. I know you can do better—let's hope so, anyway," he says.

Back at his desk, Bob shrugs, shakes his head and digs in. He thinks it's a fine project, but it isn't the first time he and the boss have disagreed. He is annoyed, but not upset.

The boss calls a female employee into his office.

"These plans just aren't going to work, Barbara. I think you have some good ideas, but they don't come together. Let's try it again. I know you can do better—let's hope so, anyway," he says.

Back at her desk, Barbara stares at the plans, while her stomach knots and her hands shake.

"I blew it. I really blew it. The project is a mess—he said so. My ideas are no good—he's right. I know he doesn't like me—I can tell. In fact, he's probably getting ready to fire me," she thinks.

Not all women would think that, and the examples are probably extreme. But the reactions they depict are fairly typical, said a psychologist who specializes in women's problems.

"Many women find it difficult to accept criticism of any kind at face value. They tend to internalize it until it becomes condemnation of themselves as people, rather than of a particular act," he said.

"And a large part of the reason is that until recently little girls were not expected to compete in any area. They never learned what it was like to strike out in a ball game, or not make the football team the first time they tried out.

"They weren't even expected to compete for high grades, generally."

121

"Little boys learned about competing early on. They learned about failure, and about coming back the next day and making a home run, too. They learned one incident doesn't mean much, if you're generally good at something," he said.

"You can't be self-confident if you don't know that. You spend too much of your time being afraid you'll make a mistake. And you can't handle making mistakes until you've had a chance to make a few."

How do we get better at taking criticism?

"With time—and practice," the psychologist said. As we feel more comfortable in competitive situations, we'll have more confidence in our own basic abilities.

As we have more opportunities to fail, as well as succeed, we'll become more comfortable making an occasional mistake.

"In the meantime, Barbara might begin forcing herself to repeat what the boss said, word for word, as soon as she gets back to her desk. She might even write it down, word for word.

"Then she can try to accept what he said—not what she thinks he meant," the psychologist said.

"He didn't *say* she blew it. He didn't *say* her ideas were no good. And he certainly didn't say he was going to fire her."

What he did say was much less alarming, if Barbara can only see it. She will. We all will—with a little practice.

Sometimes, though, the hard work, the conscientiousness, the candor just won't pay off. Why? Because there's a man standing in the doorway who refuses to let us by. It's nearly impossible to affect him—or even to run over him. A Southern woman I talked to had a subtle and devastatingly effective method of coping with this all-too-familiar type.

Her boss calls her one of the "girls." He often asks her to bring coffee. He's made it clear he thinks women with children should stay home—and makes cracks about "libbers." In short, he makes her furious a great deal of the time.

She smiles, does her job, and says nothing.

"Am I copping out? Maybe. Sometimes it even looks that way to me," she said, laughing.

"I can't believe I put up with his attitude sometimes. But I do, and I'll keep right on. You know why? Because I'm going to win, eventually. He doesn't think so, but I am."

She is the assistant manager of a branch bank in the Southeast. Her boss is the manager.

"It would be easy to blow up. I'd like to tell him just what to do with his coffee! But it wouldn't change him and it wouldn't help me, either. It would just give him something concrete to report to his boss—a reason to make my job even more impossible, or fire me," she said.

"I cannot give this man any concrete reason to put me down to his boss behind my back, when I can't defend myself. It's my boss's boss who will eventually suggest a promotion for me. I know it.

"He's already expressed an interest in my work, and he knows who I am and what I'm capable of. He's not prejudiced against women the way my boss is, either, and he's a sharp guy.

"I'm a very ambitious person," she said. "I think that's why my boss is so threatened. He suspects what I know—that I'm not going to be working in a small branch for the rest of my life.

"But he will be, you see. He's fifty now. And going nowhere. I'm thirty-three, and planning to go a lot further in this organization by the time I'm fifty.

"It's hard to keep that in mind, when he's making cracks and withholding responsibility from me. You bet it is! I've come home lots of nights just spitting nails.

"But the next day? I'm just as sweet as pie, y'all," she said, exaggerating her natural Southern accent.

"And I can do that because I know some things. I know I'm bright and very good at my job. I know he's not very bright or good at his job.

"Mostly I know I can be *his* boss someday, if I work hard, do a good job, and keep my mouth shut.

"That's how I'm going to win—not with one blast that will make me feel good for thirty seconds, but by waiting until I'm in a position of authority (and I will be, in two or three years) then watching him squirm," she said, rubbing her hands together.

"I don't care what the militants say—they could learn something from Southern women. We've been doing this for one hundred years; smiling prettily and passing up the battle so we can win the war.

"If that's copping out, or being a hypocrite, so be it. It works.

"Ten years from now I won't remember his name, or how it was (exactly) he made my life miserable. Meanwhile, I'm not going to let him goad me into 'blowing it.'

"Winning the war is much too important. And I will win, believe me!"

124

In playing the game, working women have sometimes found that no matter how well they follow the rules, no matter how well they play, they're still losing. You might just have to have the rules rewritten, and an outside referee called in to enforce them.

You've worked hard and done your best, but not much is happening. You may have been given routine raises from time to time but you haven't been promoted as fast as you think you should have been. Or you haven't been given as much responsibility as you think you can handle.

Is your employer being unfair? Are you being discriminated against because you are a woman?

A training director and Equal Employment Opportunity officer at a local bank has some concrete suggestions for the woman who suspects she's been treated unfairly.

And though he stressed throughout a lengthy interview that his views are his own and that every case should be handled differently, some of the things he had to say could apply to most women at one time or another.

"The view most companies have is that if a person feels they're being discriminated against, the company should have a shot at it first," he said.

So the first step is to go to your immediate supervisor and talk it over—a good idea even if you're absolutely sure it won't do any good.

"If you don't do that first, chances are anyone else you go to isn't going to want to discuss it. They're likely to feel that the supervisor should have been given a chance, at least, to deal with the problem," he said.

Talking to your boss about discrimination can be a

frightening thought for any woman, he admitted. You're dealing with a person whom you perceive to be un-fair—who is, you believe, "out to get you" because you're female.

And because he or she is in a position of authority, there's always the chance of recrimination—making the situation even more unbearable than it has been.

There's no guarantee that won't happen—but if the situation is bad enough to warrant action, you probably have taken the first, necessary step toward a remedy, the director said.

Obviously, a great deal will depend on how you take that step. The interview resulted in some suggestions that may prove helpful. They are:

—Don't talk about discrimination, talk about unfairness instead.

—When you're talking about unfairness, be very sure you are armed with concrete examples of it.

—Don't blame him, don't accuse. Just talk about the situation as you perceive it exists.

—Be nonemotional. Come in with a problem-solving attitude, not just a gripe.

—Be prepared before you go in. Make sure your per-formance has been up to par before you talk about unfair-ness. Make a list of your specific complaints, practice what you're going to say.

That list might entail some honest self-evaluation, too, he said.

"Companies are very result oriented. They're becoming more and more interested in production and less inter-ested in paternalism.

"If you don't have the results, if you haven't been producing, you have no right to complain if you're not promoted."

But what if, despite your best efforts, you aren't
satisfied with what your supervisor has said?

"Here, she would go to personnel. Ideally, they repre-
sent the company—not management or the employee—
and they would try to get the facts as objectively as possible."

If you have exhausted all avenues available to you
within a company, and you don't want to look for work
elsewhere, there is a final step you can take if you feel you
are being discriminated against: contact a representative
of a state or federal agency which deals with discrimination.

17

Time to Move On

The time has come for Mary to find a new job. She knows it—has for some time. Only trouble is, she can't seem to do anything about it.

Five years ago, when she entered the job market, Mary was glad she found a job at all. She was totally inexperienced, though her master's degree helped her land a job in New York with a market research firm.

"I loved the work right from the beginning. And I learned fast—enough to be promoted to the top of my department in three years. I like the people I work for (and with) too. That's not the problem," she said.

"It's just that I've gone about as far as I'm going with this company. I'm not challenged anymore. I've stopped growing, and I know it. I'm doing exactly what I was doing last year and the year before.

"Besides," she said, smiling, "I've been told I could earn a lot more somewhere else. I'm underpaid for the work I do.

"But I'm terrified. Absolutely frozen! I'm afraid I won't

even get an interview, let alone a new job. I'm afraid this company will find out I'm looking. I'm even more afraid I *will* get a new job—and I won't like it, or be any good at it, or they won't like me.

"There's this enormous temptation to leave well enough alone—this feeling that it may not be the best job in the world but at least I know all about it, and I know I can cope with it.

"I can't seem to make a move. I can't pick up the telephone to arrange an interview without my stomach knotting and my heart jumping into my throat. I've tried so many times—and hung up before I finished dialing the number," she said.

"And yet I am ambitious. My career is important to me. So why can't I find the courage to even *look* for a better opportunity? Why am I tempted to stay here forever, at my very first job?"

I asked a psychologist that question, and he had this to say:

"First of all, where in the rule books does it say you're not supposed to be afraid? There are two ways to approach fear. One is to say 'I have made a decision *but* I am afraid'—which stops you from acting. The other is to say 'I have made a decision *and* I am afraid.' One is inhibiting, the other facilitating.

"To make a decision, to seize control and act, is a frightening thing. No doubt about it.

"Men are afraid, too, when they make the decision to change jobs—of course they are. But it can be particularly difficult for a woman, because she may not be convinced she's supposed to want more. She hasn't been trained to

129

think in terms of advancement, and five-year goals, and advantageous moves, the way men in the business world have been.

"She may even have some internal sanctions—taboos—she's not fully aware of. Deep down, she may feel women aren't supposed to be ambitious, or that loyalty and service are more important than personal advancement.

"Those things she'll have to work out—with or without the help of a professional counselor. In the meantime, she might try this simple trick: I call it relabeling.

"There is a theory that the physiological reaction is really the same for fear, excitement, love, anticipation and apprehension. Certainly, knotting stomachs and jumping hearts are common symptoms of all these emotions.

"So, for a while, she might try saying to herself, 'I've made a decision, and I'm excited,' rather than 'I'm afraid.' Again, one is facilitating, the other inhibiting. Sounds simple, but often works!

"Recognizing fear isn't easy. Acting in spite of it is even more difficult. But the alternative—in this case a nonchallenging job, year after year—isn't easy, either. Compared to that, picking up the telephone is a cinch."

Another woman is intelligent, capable and ambitious. She has worked for three years and been promoted twice. Now she's been told the bank is ready to move her into a management position.

She's not sure she wants it.

"I work hard now, but I don't have a lot of responsibility—I pretty much do as I'm told. I don't have to work overtime and I don't carry the job home with me," she said.

"If I go into management, all that will change. I'll be more involved and something will have to suffer. I'm afraid my family will. So you might say I want it, but my family comes first.

"I know I can take care of them and handle the job I'm doing. I'm not so sure I can go up the corporate ladder and still take good care of them. Successful career women aren't always successful wives and mothers," she said.

I am about to climb on the old soapbox.

There is absolutely no reason to assume that success in the office will mean failure at home. There is no reason to assume we will follow the example of so many men who divorce their families to marry their careers.

The successful women I know who care about their families spend as much time with them as those who work at routine jobs. Sometimes more.

Women in positions of responsibility and authority don't punch time clocks, for one thing. Nor are they paid by the hour. They're paid for what they know, what they accomplish.

They can take a two-hour lunch break to attend an occasional school play, and not be in danger of losing their jobs. They can take a child to the doctor, too, or leave early if there is a crisis at home.

Often, theirs is the kind of work that can be done at home in a pinch—at night when the children are asleep, or during the day while a sick child recuperates. They may work more hours per week, but they have some actual control over when to work those hours.

A woman who has progressed in her career naturally earns a better salary, too. She can afford excellent child care, reliable help with housework and other conveniences that leave her more relaxed time with her family.

Finally, a successful woman may be more committed, yet less exhausted by the end of a week than a woman with a routine job. Variation, challenge and satisfaction do not tire us. Boredom does.

Some successful career women neglect their families, of course. Some women with routine jobs do, too. And so do some housewives, for that matter.

But few men deliberately lower their horizons because of their families. No one asks them if they're being fair in accepting a promotion or a raise. We need not lower our horizons, either. Those of us (too few) who have a choice can choose success—and choose not to neglect our families as well.

If we care about our families, we will care for them. We will do our share, whether we work in a factory or in the executive suite. If we want success, I think we can have it—without neglecting our children or being unfair to our husbands.

And if we believe that, we can choose whether or not to climb the ladder—without clouding the issue.

18

Sex:
A Handicap and a Danger

You're single, and reasonably attractive. You work with men. Chances are one of them will ask you for a date before long.

You've heard the stories about office involvements. They end (generally) badly. It is (generally) uncomfortable for both parties, sooner or later. If there is a loser, it is (generally) the woman—she may even lose all hope of advancement in the company.

But he's attractive, and you're attracted to him. Besides, there's not much opportunity to meet men outside the office and you're tired of eating canned spaghetti at home.

Should you do it? Is it worth it?

Most women say it is not, even if another can of spaghetti is the alternative.

"It is the ultimate no-win situation. There is just no way you're going to come out of it without losing," said a thirty-four-year-old administrative assistant who "tried it once or twice, years ago."

Another veteran of several office dating situations agreed. "You can do it, but you'd better know ahead of time that you're going to lose—one way or the other," she said.

"Even if you are the most mature people in the world; even if you can date, then stop dating and remain friends; even if neither of you tells a soul—you're going to lose.

"Why? Because, like or not, other people in the office are going to know about it. You may as well face that. And once it's over you will be treated differently by the people around you—men and women.

"It's a double standard and it's not fair, but it's true. He'll get kidded and winked at; you'll get cold silences," she said.

Still another woman said she "knew the affair I had might jeopardize my chances with the company. And it did; before the involvement was over, it ruined them completely.

"Management doesn't like to see that kind of thing going on between workers. And if anyone is going to be blamed, you can be pretty sure it will be the woman."

A woman who eventually became engaged to the co-worker she dated said the fact they worked in the same office eventually ruled the relationship.

"There was no respite; we were around each other day and night and that leads to complications. If he saw me smiling and talking on the telephone, he wanted to know who I was talking to. If he didn't smile as he walked by, I thought he was upset about something. It was a mess, and it finally broke us up," she said.

And a woman who has "never tried it, though I've come close" said she couldn't imagine dating a coworker, even if a deeper relationship did not result from it.

"You can't date someone, even once or twice, and not have your personal life exposed. I draw a clear line between my personal and professional life, because I am a professional. That wouldn't be possible after the second date, and then I'd have to deal with him every day on some level," she said.

So, for many working people, it seems safest to avoid office dating. As one woman put it, "there are lots of men out there who won't complicate my life and threaten my job. Why not date them instead?"

The question of dating someone in the office crops up frequently. Fortunately, it can usually be handled with tact. But there is another, more serious problem relating to sex in the office—the boss, or fellow employee, who won't accept *no* to his sexual advances.

"He was fatherly and kind, at first, and seemed to take an interest in my work. He told me I had a lot of potential. I was so inexperienced I needed all the help I could get. He was the boss, and I guess I was flattered," she said.

"Then he began to make it clear he had more than a paternal interest in me. I tried to ignore the sexual innuendos, I tried to look and act professional at all times; I did all the things you're supposed to do but they didn't work. He got more and more insistent."

She accepted a job with another company. "It wasn't really a good move for me, but I just couldn't take it any longer."

"You cannot win," another woman said. "If you give in you'll lose and if you say no you'll lose, too.

"I've never had a problem with the men in my office;

135

but my clients are another story! A man in my business can wine and dine clients—but some of them expect a lot more from a woman. Generally, talking about my husband and kids avoids out-and-out propositions, but there have been times when that hasn't worked, either.

"I know I've lost at least three good clients because I' said 'no' and hurt their egos. And that's so unfair," she said.

Sexual interplay between consenting adults is not what these women are talking about. What they *are* talking about is sexual harassment—one-sided, unwelcomed, persistent advances from the men with whom they must work.

If you've faced this problem, you are not alone. In a recent survey of 9,000 working women, taken by *Redbook* magazine, nearly nine out of ten women said they had experienced sexual harassment of some kind while trying to do their jobs.

If the harassment comes from a coworker, it can be annoying and embarrassing. If it comes from a supervisor or client (someone with the power to reward and punish) it can spell real disaster to the woman who cares about her job.

Too often, we say nothing. Too often, we're afraid of causing a scene, or looking foolish, or ruining our chances of advancement within the company.

"I worked for a man who was fifty years old and married. I was twenty-four and single. He made my life an absolute hell on earth for a year and I was afraid to tell anyone. His boss was a man, too. I figured they'd stick together and I'd end up looking silly and be out of a job, as well," a woman now thirty and married said, shaking her head.

"He called me into his office several times a week, then talked about his frigid wife, and how attractive I was—I'm sure you get the picture. And he was all over me—leaning, squeezing my arm, touching my leg. It was really sickening.

"I finally asked to be transferred to another department, just to get away from him. I felt victimized, very angry inside. But I never told a soul.

"I wish I had, now," she added. "He's still there and I'm sure he has another victim, by now."

Perhaps his newest victim will find the courage to tell him, in no uncertain terms, that she does not appreciate his attentions. If he continues to harass her (or retaliates unfairly) perhaps she will report him to his supervisor—armed with a carefully kept diary of specific offenses and when they occurred.

And if that doesn't work, perhaps she will file a complaint with her city or state Commission on Human Rights or Fair Employment Practices agency. She may even complain to the federally-funded Equal Employment Opportunity Commission (EEOC) office in her area.

Taking action against this particular man may, sadly, not accomplish much. She may still prefer to resign rather than deal with him every day. She may run into a similar problem in the next office. And she may continue to feel angry, unreasonably guilty, and rather helpless in the face of sexual harassment on the job.

137

But realizing she is not alone may help. And taking action of some kind—refusing to be victimized—must be a step in the right direction. For all of us.

Sooner or later, most working women end up eating dinner alone in a restaurant, or spending a night alone in a hotel.

Betty Friedan, Margaret Mead, Barbara Walters and Margaret Chase Smith all say they have a problem with it. And so do I.

Traditionally, men have been prepared to travel now and then, as they move up the corporate ladder, and to work late and dine alone.

Now women, as we move into managerial positions in increasing numbers, must be prepared to do the same. And a woman has three strikes against her before she starts.

The first is that men have a way of assuming any woman alone must be dying for company—their company. Not all men are guilty, of course, but enough so that a woman traveling alone must be prepared for unwelcome advances.

The second is that maitre d's and hotel clerks have a way of prejudging a woman alone, too—which can lead to sneers, sly glances and, sometimes, outright rudeness.

And the third is that most of us are aware of the first two—which makes us feel uncomfortable before we ever walk into the restaurant or check into the hotel.

Solutions? Most women find it helps to bring something to read when they eat out alone. It doesn't matter what, it just gives them something to *do*.

And if you want a cocktail, before or during dinner, veterans say order it at your table or through room service, never in the hotel's lounge.

"I travel two or three days a month in my job and I just plan my day so I'm back in my room by dark; then I don't go out again, for anything," said a young woman who works for a college endowment fund.

"I use room service like mad. What you're ordering may cost a bit more, but my company understands," she said. "I'm safer doing that, and it avoids the whole restaurant hassle."

For a woman alone, it's especially important to make reservations whenever possible, experienced travelers say. "Never go to a restaurant without a reservation. And never, never try to register at a hotel unless you've called ahead. When you do call, make it clear that you will be dining alone, too. If the maitre d' is cool or unpleasant, find another restaurant," one veteran traveler said flatly. "I do. It isn't worth going just to prove a point. I don't enjoy the meal if I feel unwelcome, so why stay?"

Finally, if you are annoyed by unwelcome attention from anyone, don't put up with it.

"Make it clear you prefer to be left alone. If that doesn't work, complain. Tell the head waiter, the hotel clerk, or, if all else fails, find a policeman. You may feel foolish, but you have a right to privacy, a right to be left alone," one woman said.

"And a lot of women get into serious trouble because they didn't want to cause a scene. You have a right to travel alone, unmolested. Assert it."

Besides dating, fighting off the office Casanova, and traveling alone, perhaps the most traumatic sexual problem of them all is rape.

139

You have a lot of things on your mind as you cross the parking lot, heading for home after a hard day's work. Rape is not one of them. But in New York City alone, in 1975, more than 3,800 women learned it could happen to them.

Any woman is a potential victim. Working women—who shop at night, commute alone during evening hours, and work late shifts in large cities—are particularly vulnerable.

But Lieutenant Mary Keese, commanding officer of the New York City Police Department's Sex Crimes Analysis Unit, says there are some rules any working woman should follow, to minimize the risk of attack.

They are:

—Leave the office with a coworker, whenever possible. If you must walk to your car (or to public transportation) go with someone. "Rapists generally look for a lone victim," Keese said.

—If you drive home from work, keep your car doors locked at all times. And if you give someone a ride (never a stranger!) be sure and lock your car doors again, as soon as he or she gets out of the car.

—When parking your car, be sure you're under a light of some kind. Park as close to your building as possible, even if it costs a bit more. And always check your car before you get back in, although you may feel sure you locked it eight hours earlier.

—If you ride elevators, try not to do so alone. Wait until at least one other woman arrives, if possible. And never get into an elevator containing someone who looks suspicious. "Don't worry about being rude. Politeness gets a lot of women into serious trouble," said Lieutenant Keese.

—If you live in an apartment building, have your key ready before you get to your door, so you can enter quickly and lock the door behind you. If you notice a stranger loitering in the hallway (and you live alone) don't try to enter your apartment. Go to someone nearby, if possible, and ask them to come with you to your apartment.

—If you live in a residential area, and you think you're being followed, pull into your driveway but do not get out of your car. Blow your horn until help comes. And in the meantime, remember a locked car is the safest place you can be.

—If you are walking to a bus, train or subway stay on the well-lit side of the street or take a well-lit busy route—even if it takes a little longer. Crowds and light are good defenses against attack; and a shortcut may turn out to be much more trouble than it's worth.

—If a man asks you for directions from his car, do not walk over to him. If he speaks too softly, stand where you are and ask him to speak louder. This is a common ploy, Keese said. Many women have been pulled into cars and raped because they tried to be polite and helpful.

—Finally, never be reluctant to cause a scene if you feel threatened in any way.

"This may be the most important advice I can give," Keese said. "We women have been taught to be polite, to avoid being rude at all cost. It can cost us a lot.

"It's better to cause a terrible scene and be wrong than to take an unnecessary chance. For a rape victim, the price of being polite is very, very high."

141

19

Your Child's Sickness and Your Own

Your child is sick. It's seven o'clock in the morning. You have to be at work in an hour, you have no one to stay with her, and now you're going to have to make that dreaded phone call.

"I'm so sorry, but I just can't leave her alone. Hopefully she'll be better by tomorrow and I can come back to work. I'll let you know."

But she isn't better by tomorrow, or the next day, or the next.

"What do I do then? I panic," said a commercial artist who has three young children.

"I remember about a year ago when my daughter (now 4 years old) had one ear infection after another. My boss was really great about it—he kept telling me not to worry, that he knew she had to come first.

"But I kept thinking of all the people in the office who don't have to stay home when a child is sick, and I always wondered if he was thinking about that, too," she said.

That concern seems to be a common one, and several

women have told me they feel it more now that the economic situation is still making competition for jobs keen.

"If you have sick kids and have to be home with them, then you're obviously not producing as much as the men and the women without families are," said one, who works for a large insurance agency.

There haven't been any memos or directives, she said. "It's just an attitude, and you can sense it. It's a cold silence when you say you can't make it in to work. It's remarks that are made if you have to leave early to take a child to the doctor—that kind of thing."

There doesn't seem to be a standard solution to the sick-child problem; each woman I talked to seemed to have a different one or no answer at all.

What do you do if you don't have family close by, or a husband with a flexible schedule, or a reliable woman who will come without prior notice? If you're like I am, you probably worry a lot and "play it by ear," when it happens.

But several women have said there are some things you can do even if the worst happens and you're home for a week. It's a matter of attitude—that can make all the difference. First, you've got to assume the boss realized you might be out now and then when he hired you. He knew you had children, after all. So, while you may feel bad about it, don't apologize every two minutes, they said.

Offer to do some work at home, if that's feasible. Perhaps you can find someone to stay with your child for just a few hours a day. If so, hire her. Then offer to come in to work for those few hours. It's better than nothing, several women with children pointed out.

143

Offer to work some overtime, once your child is well, to help make up for the time you lost. Again, do it in a positive, rather than apologetic, way.

One male employer, who supervises fifteen women in his office said, "If she has children and they're sick, I understand she'll probably have to stay home with them.

"But I feel a lot better about the women who seem to have things under control. It's the ones who call up and say, 'I'm sorry, there's nothing I can do. I don't know when I'll be back' that get my goat."

"Their attitude seems to be that it's my problem, not theirs," he said.

It isn't easy to have a positive attitude when you're worried about a sick child and about your job at the same time.

But it isn't the boss's problem, after all, it's ours. We can't stop children from getting sick, but we can let our employers know that we care, and we're doing everything possible to handle the job—to make it easier for him.

In recent years, much has been written about doctor-patient relationships. But working women have special needs, sometimes not met by physicians, and little has been written about them.

We need to be taken seriously, first of all; to be treated as mature, responsible adults rather than little girls. A pat on the head is no substitute for solid information.

If we are mothers, we need to be given credit for common sense and sound judgment. We are not diagnosticians, of course. But we can tell the difference between a child with a headcold who needs a decongestant, and one who should see the doctor.

When physicians insist on office visits, no matter what the symptoms, they force us to take unnecessary time away from our jobs. And we have enough trouble taking necessary time off!

Speaking of time, we don't have much of it. We cannot afford to spend two hours in a waiting room before a routine doctor's appointment. Few male executives would tolerate such treatment. Working women cannot tolerate it, either.

Nearly half of all the women in this country now work. But family doctors, pediatricians, dentists and orthodontists still close their offices by 4:00 P.M., generally, and seldom have regular Saturday office hours.

That places a burden on all patients who work—and a double burden on working mothers who must find time for their children's medical needs, as well as their own.

Someday, perhaps, "regular" hours for physicians will be from noon to seven o'clock, four days a week and all day Saturday. In the meantime, we desperately need understanding doctors and receptionists who will schedule nonemergency appointments late in the day, or first thing in the morning.

A 4:30 P.M. doctor's appointment means leaving work early; but a 10:00 A.M. appointment means most of our morning is wasted. And we have no time to waste.

Working women need physicians sympathetic to their situation. It is no help to be told we should "quit and stay home" when we are worried about a sick child, or if we are tired or ill ourselves. Doctors do not routinely suggest their male patients "quit and stay home," after all. And we cope with enough guilt as it is.

We need physicians who will take our problems

145

seriously—really listen to us—and who are aware of the enormous demands on our physical and emotional energies.

And how can I ask all that of a busy doctor? Because my own family physician fills those needs. It took two years to find him; but it was worth it. A working relationship with an understanding physician is invaluable to any working woman.

If your own doctor makes your job more difficult, it may be time to have an honest talk with him. And if that doesn't help, it may be time to look for another doctor.

My family doctor scolded me a few days ago. And he was right. I thought I'd pass along what he had to say— just in case some of you are guilty, too.

He said working mothers are his "worst" patients. We surpass even high-pressure male executives in lack of common sense about our own health, he fumed.

"If your children are sick, you bring them in right away. If your husband isn't well, you call and make an appointment for him. But you don't seem to think you can get sick, just like everyone else.

"Most of you don't get enough sleep, or the right kind of exercise. When you are ill, you drag yourself to work for weeks, instead of staying in bed three days and getting well," he said.

"And when you do see a doctor, you expect us to cure you in four hours so you can get back to the office. I'm just a physician, not a miracle worker.

"I have women come in here and say they're tired, they don't have any energy. And they want me to do something about it. But when I find out what their lives are like, I just shake my head.

"Of course they're tired! Who wouldn't be, going fourteen and sixteen hours a day, not eating properly, not getting enough rest? There's no magic pill for that, I'm afraid," he said.

It is difficult indeed to stay home with a cold or the flu if you feel guilty because you were home a month ago when Junior had it. It seems easier to go to work sick than lie in bed and wonder what your boss and your coworkers are thinking of you.

Most working fathers can afford to stay home sick, from time to time—they generally haven't missed a certain number of days already because the children were ill and needed them.

Overwhelmingly, it's the working woman in the family who stays home when a child is sick, or leaves the office early if there is a medical or dental appointment made.

But we work for, share offices with, and compete against those same men who need not take time away from their careers because of a sick child, or a child-care snafu. It makes the competition tough, I think.

And (if we care about our jobs) it can make us defensive enough to neglect our own health care, rather than take more time away from the office.

Perhaps we can learn, from those male executives the doctor mentioned. We've watched some of them suffer from ulcers and heart attacks, alienate families and neglect their own health and happiness, all in the name of "getting ahead."

Maybe we should let the cobwebs gather, while we relax at home a bit, and remember our employers knew we were working mothers when they hired us, and knew we would have to be home, from time to time, if our

147

children were ill. They knew, too, that everyone must stay home, sometimes, with his or her own illness.

The more I think about it, the better it sounds. I can hardly wait for my next bad headcold!

20

She Refused to Make Coffee at the Office

Iris Rivera doesn't see herself as a radical, or a women's libber. But in January 1977, she refused to obey a rule, because she thought it unfair and demeaning. She was fired from her job because of that refusal.

The rule required secretaries in the Illinois State Appellate Defenders office to prepare coffee for their bosses, each day.

A small, insignificant issue?

"Not at all," said Mrs. Rivera, in Chicago. "I know a lot of secretaries make coffee, and that wasn't the real issue. It's that it was stated as a rule, not a request. That was demeaning to me, as a person. That was wrong.

"I feel I support my kids, I take care of them at home, and I have my job at the office. I don't take my job home, and I shouldn't have to be a homemaker in the office.

"Next, they'll tell me to sweep the floor—and there's nothing wrong with sweeping floors, I don't mean to imply that. There's nothing wrong with making coffee, either. It just isn't my job," she said.

Mrs. Rivera is a thirty-five-year-old widow who supports three sons, twelve, ten, and five years old. As a secretary in the Defender's office, she brought home $160 a week.

"The rule was in a memo from my boss—Deputy Defender James Geif, and I took it home. I thought about it all night, and the next day I went to see Mr. Geif and asked if we could negotiate on the rule about making coffee," she said.

"He said absolutely not. So I said I would not be making coffee, although the five other secretaries in my office had agreed to do so.

"That afternoon, he came to my desk and said I was fired and had two weeks notice—in front of everyone in the office," she said.

Mrs. Rivera filed suit through the state Fair Employment Practice Commission, asking that her job be reinstated and that any salary she lost while the matter is pending be paid back to her. She did not ask for damages.

In the meantime, she wondered how she would care for her children.

"I told them right away. I told them I'd been fired, and why, and they just said I should stand up for what I think is right. They're with me all the way. . . ." Her voice trailed off, and she sighed.

"This has just overwhelmed me, I guess. I'm just a common working type, looking out for my children. I don't belong to a lot of women's groups and I don't think of myself as a feminist.

"I work all day, and come home and cook supper, maybe do a load of wash, and I'm usually in bed before ten. I don't even watch the news! Now, all of a sudden,

150

everybody's interested in this thing. And all I was doing was trying to have some self-respect, for myself—not for any cause," she said.

"But men are husbands and fathers, and no one asks them to be homemakers at the office. Why should there be this assumption that it's different for me, because I'm a woman?

"I can't change the big things that are wrong, maybe, but I think you have to start with the small ones first, the ones that are important to you as a person.

"I don't know what will happen now. I hope I'll get my job back, or find another one quickly. I hope people won't label me as a troublemaker; I hope someone will hire me based on my abilities.

"One of my sons has a birthday coming up, and there won't be one if I'm unemployed. But I believe in what I'm doing, and that's important, too."

When I talked to her again, three months later, Iris Rivera was alone, in the hospital, and could not afford to feed her children.

Her cause had become a national news story, and she appealed her case to Ted Gottfried, the head of the agency, who reversed the decision.

That was in January. But before she knew she had "won," Mrs. Rivera, thirty-five, found herself in an emergency room and then in an operating room undergoing major surgery. She didn't hear the news until the operation was over.

She went through two more operations, was in the hospital over two months, and had received no income of any kind for almost two months.

Although a friend was keeping the children, Mrs. Riv-

151

era had been sending checks to cover their food, clothing and incidental expenses. Her friend could not afford to keep feeding them, she told me.

"State employees who are out of work for more than thirty days are entitled to nonoccupational disability benefits—half one's normal salary," she said.

"I thought I would get a check in March. I got forms, instead. I filled them out. My physicians filled them out. Nothing happened. Finally, I learned I should have received a different form—an application form.

"Finally, I got it. And I sent it back last week; but I've been told it will be at least three or four weeks before it can be processed. That's some time in May. And right now, I can't feed my kids."

"I had no savings account, but I did have a checking account and was writing checks to pay for my sons' food. Now, I have six dollars left, and I don't know what I am going to do," she said softly.

She called the Public Aid office in Chicago. "They said I would be eligible for emergency aid, but that I couldn't get any until I could come in and fill out forms. That really wasn't much help! I can't come; I'm in the hospital," she said.

"When I went in for the first operation, I said 'Walk with me a little longer, Lord, because I have my sons to take care of.' He did, and if I didn't have my faith I'd never get through this. I've been praying a lot, and having faith in God. That's about all I can do, right now," she said.

"My mother lives in Iowa and is taking care of her

ninety-three-year-old father, who is ill. She can't help, I know.

"Right now, the problems in the office seem pretty far away. I didn't even know I'd won until after I had the first operation. Now, all I want to do is get well and get back to work so I can take care of my sons. . . ."

"I just wish the state would hurry things up a little," she said, from her $137-a-day semiprivate room in Chicago's Grant Hospital.

Mrs. Rivera did have group medical insurance, but it did not pay all of her medical bills. "I've been told the bill for three months here and three major operations already is around $50,000. It may well be more by the time I get out, and I'll have to handle that as best I can," she said.

"I don't want anything but what is rightfully mine. I don't want donations or anything else like that—I only want the $400 a month in disability the state owes me. And then I just want to get well and go back to work.

"It's so hard to go through something like this as a widow. Your friends tend to stop coming after the first few weeks. And there's no one out there to take care of things until I can get well."

Attorney Steven Clark, in the State Appellate Defender's Office, said he, too, had called the pension system in the state's capital to "see what the problem was."

"They said they had nothing on her—no file—at first. When I insisted and called our offices down there, someone did find her file," he said.

"But the real problem is bureaucratic red tape. The wheels of the bureaucracy turn terribly slowly, and the

153

red tape is taking a while to get untangled."

"We wish Iris Rivera well. Five of us (out of thirteen attorneys) have given blood for her—and two others tried to. But hurrying up the bureaucracy? I don't know if anyone can do that," he added.

PART IV

Recognizing Our Needs and the Needs of Others

21

Handling Our Loneliness

"If one more person tells me to get out and start dating, I'll scream!"

Faded freckles, faded blond hair, tired eyes.

"When would I date, for heaven's sake? I have three little kids, no husband, and I work two jobs just to make ends meet. The kids are in bed by the time I get home. That leaves weekends for them," she said.

"I spend all day Saturday trying to run fifty errands in eight hours—and Sunday washing clothes and cooking ahead so the sitter can feed the kids halfway decent meals the next week."

She is thirty-five years old and has been alone for two years. Her children are three, four and six years old. She is a department store clerk full time and a waitress part time. She looks forty-five.

"See," she leaned forward, "I work the night job so I can pay a sitter, so I can work during the day. Now isn't that something? I'm on this merry-go-round, you might say. . . .

"There are no day-care centers near where I live—they're all in the good sections. And I can't afford to live where they are.

"That means paying a girl twice what I can afford to come and keep the kids. What else can I do? They sure aren't old enough to look out for themselves! And they won't be until I'm past forty years old. "If I last that long," she said, shaking her head.

"There used to be a day-care center down the street from me—Head Start. But they closed it up about two years ago. I don't know why. 'Course, that was when I was still married, and he hadn't got tired of the whole thing and took off. . . ."

Her husband "took off" two years ago, saying he would look for work in Baltimore, 400 miles away. She hasn't heard from him since.

"I don't know where he is. His own Mama doesn't know where he is. What am I going to do? Get the cops after him? A lot of good that would do," she said.

"I'm not married and I'm not single—though I guess I'm a lot more single than anything else. It isn't that, makes me not date men. It's just that I got no time—for anything."

She stopped for breath, ordered another cup of coffee, and insisted on paying for it.

"You can leave the tip; I always feel bad when I can't," she said.

"I'll tell you something. I got people at work always trying to fix me up with someone. For a date, you know? Well, if just once someone would offer to take care of the kids, I might just take them up on it.

"My Mama used to take the kids, sometimes, but she

had a stroke a while back and now she's in a nursing home across town. I don't get to see her much, even, because they don't allow kids in there. Besides, I can't afford the bus fare too often.

"Hell, I don't know if I'd date anyway," she said. "Don't know if I'd want to be with a man now. Being with one got me in enough trouble as it is. I sure don't need to look for more. . . .

She's a working woman, and she needs help.

"You've been real nice," she said, a crumpled list of agencies in one hand, and tears in her eyes. "I haven't talked this much in a year! And I'll think about what you said about getting help.

"Thanks for hearing me out—it sure was good to talk to somebody."

Another woman didn't even have time to be lonely. She was too busy just surviving.

"When my husband and I separated, I knew I had to find a job—fast. I did. I also had to learn how to mow lawns, fix leaky pipes, repair the kids' toys, balance a checkbook and manage a budget," she said.

"I had to learn not to cry all the time, too. I couldn't let the kids see how really frightened and miserable I was. Just surviving—keeping things together, holding a full-time job and taking care of two youngsters—kept me too busy to be lonely."

She survived that first year. And the second.

"But now it's not enough. I'm tired of Saturday nights, Sunday nights alone. And Tuesday nights, Wednesday nights—all my nights, in fact," she said.

"And I'm not talking about dating. Romance is the last

thing I need right now. I'm talking about friends, like you have when you're half of a married couple. Someone to call if I'm feeling lonely. Someone who will call me if she's feeling lonely. Someone to laugh with, cry with, have fun with. . . .

"Where do you find friends if you have no time left?

"I spend my evenings and weekends with the children because they need me and I'm away eight hours every day. They're only five and seven, and I'm all they have now. Their father lives 1,000 miles from here.

"But there just isn't any time left for me! By the time I do the work of two parents—run twenty errands, take one to baseball practice and one to the dentist, take them to the park, read to them, play with them, talk to them, listen to them, pick up after them . . ."

She stabbed at the ashtray with her cigarette. Then looked up, eyes brimming with tears.

"I'm so lonely I talk to the people at work even though we're not really friends. They know all about my life, although I know very little about theirs. When they go downstairs for a coffee break, I always go. Not for coffee. Just to talk. When we have lunch, I find myself talking about the children and the problems at home. They may look bored, but I rattle on anyway," she said, shaking her head.

"I know I shouldn't, but I can't seem to stop it. I have to talk to someone! And I never see other adults except at work.

"Really, the women there are mostly married and involved with their own families; or dating a lot and not very interested in women friends. And the men? I haven't met one yet who just wanted to be a friend.

"I don't make enough money to pay a babysitter on a regular basis. That leaves out taking a course and joining a discussion group of some kind—two things I'd like to do.

"So where do you go if you just need a friend? I wish I knew," she said, softly. "Loneliness. It's the worst thing in the world. The worst . . . "

It seems I am the only working woman I know who is, from time to time, disorganized, unproductive, inefficient—in short, all over the lot.

Such feelings are especially likely to occur when I find seven unmatched socks under the sofa and realize all of them are two sizes smaller than anything my children wear now.

Watching my children do their homework on paper napkins because, for the fourth time, I forgot to buy notebook paper on the way home doesn't help, either.

There must be other working mothers out there who haven't made a PTA meeting in three months and whose children view with alarm any cake that doesn't have a bakery's name stamped on it.

I haven't met them.

The working mothers I meet at parties tend to sip white wine, wave one hand vaguely and murmur something to the effect that yes, they do have children.

Then they change the subject.

The more I try to get down to the old nitty-gritty, the more esoteric they become.

Ask them how in the world they find time to speak to their children (let alone help them with new math, which no one seems to understand anyway), and they say,

"We-e-el-l-l, it's the quality of time spent with children that's important, not the quantity. Don't you think so?"

Of course I think so. Everyone thinks so. It would be un-American not to think so. But that doesn't make it any easier to explain new math while the phone is ringing, the baby's crying and the TV dinner is burning in the oven.

I'm guilty, too. I play the same game of putting up a cool, in-control front. Most of us do it to a greater or lesser degree.

And I think the reason is that we're just a little defensive about being working mothers in the first place—no matter how much we chant "quality of time, not quantity."

Because we are working mothers, we think we have to be perfect mothers—at least in the eyes of the outside world. That way, no one can insinuate that our children are missing something because we work. No one can make us feel guilty.

When I was a housewife with two toddlers under foot I could drop in on friends who also were housewives. They had all the problems I had—boredom, frustration, loneliness, doubt over whether they were handling their children as well as they could. But often a cup of coffee and an hour of sharing those worries made them more manageable.

We shared the problems and often the solutions to them. We didn't seem so intent on keeping up a front, on being "professional" at all times.

I know for a fact that many of us who work share similar problems.

Yet much of the reaction I get from women concerns their feelings of isolation and loneliness—of having no one with whom they can share their frustrations and worries.

Sadly, working women with families tend to have little time to talk on the telephone or have a cup of coffee with anyone. We're generally much too busy doing what has to be done each day.

But when we do find a minute, perhaps we can begin to let down some barriers, to be a little less defensive with each other.

If we can level with each other, I think we can learn from each other. And if we can learn from each other, the day may come when we won't have to be defensive— with anyone.

We sometimes misjudge just how content others are in their lives. And I found this especially true in my feelings about single women who didn't have the concerns I had to face every day.

Just thinking about a single woman can turn a working wife and mother into a resentful witch! *She* leaves the office without a care, until the next day. *She* has no one to worry about but herself. *She* has one fulltime job, not two.

When the sitter quits and Junior is home with the flu and the washing machine breaks, it's easy to imagine her flitting from one night spot to the next, always on the arm of a charming, debonair male who somehow isn't at all like the husbands *we* know.

I said all that to a single friend. Then waited while she

laughed. "You sound like those magazines! I just love the articles about cocktail parties and intimate little dinners, martini lunches and chic little ski lodges for the weekend. Good grief! If I just had someone to come home to—anyone—I'd be ecstatic," she said.

For the record, friend does not weigh 300 pounds and have two heads. She is twenty-six, attractive, bright and ambitious—good company, too. But the telephone doesn't ring and she's been eating frozen dinners for a long time now—alone.

"I work late because I don't want to come home to this empty apartment. When I do get home, I feed my dog, watch television and go to bed. Period. That's it. On weekends I stay busy doing laundry, cleaning, taking walks with the dog, sometimes going to a movie with a girlfriend. Usually I'm glad when Monday comes—at least I have somewhere to go and there are people around," she said.

There are males in her office, but she has made a firm decision not to date them. ("That's dumb—it's not worth the hassle and my job is too important to me.") There are males living near her, but they're married. ("Who needs *that* mess!")

Hands on her hips, she said, "So where does that leave me? Where do I meet men? I can't just pick them up off the street. The only advice I get is to join a church or go to singles bars. I'm not interested in joining a church, and I'm not comfortable walking into bars and restaurants alone. Does that mean I'll live alone the rest of my life?"

Then she described a working wife and mother's life, from her point of view.

"You know that no matter what happens at the office, you're not alone. If you're down, or upset, there's someone there who cares about you—your husband.

"You're the most important person in the world to your children—and that's true whether you're fat or skinny, rich or poor, a success or a failure. It doesn't matter to them, they'll still love you no matter what.

"I know you get tired with a career and a family. But I'm tired too. Of being alone, and being lonely," she said.

"There may be some swinging singles out there who are having a ball. But I know a lot more like me who are scrambling and scraping and living alone. And sometimes that just isn't much fun at all."

Suddenly, having no one to worry about but myself didn't seem quite so enviable, and not at all glamorous. The next time there's Cap'n Crunch glued to my hair rollers, I'll try to remember that.

22

. . . But No Time for Ourselves

Anne has time for her job, husband, children and friends. She has time to entertain, go out to dinner with her husband, attend her sons' ball games and (with her family's help) keep the house reasonably clean.

What she doesn't have time for is herself.

"There's absolutely nothing wrong with me; I haven't a real complaint. I just feel like crawling into a cave and not coming out," she said.

A cave?

"Sure! Quiet and dark and no one around to bug me. I could listen to the water drip, count the stones on the floor, maybe not even do that much—it sounds fantastic.

"I love working and I love my work. But I have to be frightfully organized or nothing gets done and there never seems to be time left over for me—just me," she said.

"There's always something I should be doing when I'm home. I feel I should be thinking about my family, spending all my time with them.

"It seems terribly selfish to say 'okay—I've been away from you all week but I'm *still* going to lock myself in the bedroom with a good book, today. Leave me alone!' "

I think many of us have the same problem, though some have found ingenious ways of finding time alone.

"My one luxury is having my hair done every week—and I couldn't care less about my hair! It's just an hour I can spend every Saturday morning doing absolutely nothing," wrote a woman in Dallas.

"I don't have to talk to anyone and I don't have to worry about the impression I'm making. That lovely hum from the dryer drowns out the rest of the world."

A woman in Chicago says she looks forward to the nearly two hours a day she must spend on a commuter train. "No one can ask me to do anything and there's no telephone. I don't read or make out shopping lists or talk. I spend the time sorting out my thoughts, listening to my own insides. Instead of resenting the time commuting takes out of my life, I relish it. It's my time! I don't know how I would survive without it," she said.

A Florida woman heads for the garden, when she needs time alone. "I'd feel guilty if I just withdrew from my family. But working in my garden lets me relax without the guilt. My family enjoys the vegetables I grow, and the time I spend out there alone lets me face the world, again," she wrote.

Finally, there are some able to "level" with families about their need to be alone.

"My husband and I have a deal: Saturday mornings are his, Sunday mornings are mine," wrote a Californian.

"Saturday morning he can stay upstairs with a cup of

167

coffee and the newspaper, or play golf, or sleep late—
whatever he wants, while I spend time with the kids.

"On Sunday mornings after church, I have the same
privilege. I usually spend the time alone upstairs, writing
letters or reading, or just puttering around doing nothing.
Sometimes I go for a drive—alone," she said.

"And sometimes, I feel like being with my husband
and the kids. But just knowing I can have the time if I
want it makes all the difference in the world."

Saturday. Time for jeans and T-shirts, straight hair and
no make-up. What a luxury!

But for most working women, Saturday is also the day
for shopping, laundry, cleaning, cooking and yard
work—all generally neglected during the week.

Susan has what she thinks is a better idea. For her,
Saturdays are play-days; time for sleeping late, relaxing
over a cup of coffee, tennis games, long walks in the
woods and, most importantly, hours spent with her husband and two young daughters. "I used to get up early
and spend the whole day running to stores, doing laundry, cleaning the house and feeling like a real martyr,"
she laughed.

"Not any more. Now everyone spends a little time each
evening, doing what has to be done around the house.
And I actually look forward to weekends, instead of
dreading them."

She's the first to admit her house isn't exactly spotless.
"But who cares? It's never really dirty, either. It just isn't
clean all at the same time, the way it was when I stayed
home full time.

"As a housewife, I got used to doing most chores on a once-a-week basis. Then I kept it up, when I went to work. I was a real witch by Saturday afternoon—barking orders and running from one chore to another.

"Bob and I usually hired a sitter and went out Saturday night, but by eight o'clock I was so tired I just wanted to crawl in bed—so that wasn't much fun, either. And Bob was no help at all. He refused to give up his golf games, just sat around while I ran my head off. I was ready to throttle him every weekend," she said. "Finally, I blew up. I told him I was sick and tired of working all week and working all weekend, too."

He listened, then said he agreed with her completely. He said it was absolutely ridiculous for anyone to work all weekend. And he, for one, didn't intend to do it.

"He said he would not spend his Saturdays doing chores, but he'd be more than willing to spend some time each evening, doing what had to be done," Susan said.

"Then we had a conference with the girls (ages seven and nine) and asked if they would help, too, so we could all play on the weekends. They agreed, and we assigned them specific chores to be done after school. Then, at night, Bob and I spent a little time cleaning and picking up around the house."

Within a month, Susan felt like a different woman. "I couldn't believe the difference it made in my attitude—about the housework, and about my job, too. I began to look forward to weekends, instead of dreading them. I went back to work on Mondays a lot more rested and ready to dig in. And Bob and I actually enjoyed being together again on weekends," she said.

Now the only inflexible rule in their house is "No work on Saturdays." "No matter what, we play together that one day. If it isn't done by Saturday, it doesn't get done until the next week. I don't think anyone will remember, twenty years from now, if the bathrooms were always immaculate or not.

"But I think all of us will remember the fun we've had together, now that Saturdays are play-days."

Susan and her husband have worked out an arrangement that seems most satisfying. My husband and I tried another approach that worked well for us.

One week, just the two of us. Camping on an island off the coast of Maine. Forest and ocean, cool breezes and, most of all, blissful, needed silence.

No children, no pets, telephones, doorbells, no responsibilities. Time for quiet walks and long talks, time to look inside, to find ourselves again. And each other. And, at the end, a solemn vow: to do this again, each year. Somehow.

How long has it been, since you've had a time all to yourself? If you're like most working women, it's probably been a while. There's so much to do, and so little time in which to do it. We give our time to husbands, children, careers, friends, chores and even worthy causes. But not to ourselves—and we're a worthy cause too, after all.

We are so busy taking care of others, we forget that. And the ones we care for suffer because of it.

It wasn't easy to leave the children behind. By the time we delivered them to relatives, a massive case of the guilties threatened to overwhelm this working mother.

"How can I want to get away, when I'm away from them all day? Is this irresponsible, selfish? Will they understand, or will they feel unloved, unwanted? Do parents have a right to a week alone, when we have just two vacation weeks a year?"

The answers came, on that island. It is our children who are reaping the benefits of that week, right now. And it is they who suffered because I didn't do it years ago.

A week away won't solve all the problems, or take away the hassles. My children still aren't angels, my husband still hates sharing the housework, and it's had no effect at all on the boss. But if I'm rested and relaxed I can cope better with all of them—and myself, as well.

We talk about the quality of time spent with our families being more important than the quantity. But unless we take time for ourselves, the quality is bound to suffer.

It doesn't have to be an island off the coast of Maine. It can be a tent in the woods, a shack on the beach, or a hotel room, three blocks from home. If it can't be a week, several weekends a year may work just as well.

It's the time that's important—time to be ourselves, for ourselves. For those of us who juggle at least two full-time jobs every day, it's absolutely essential.

23

When Self-Sacrifice Is No Longer Noble

Your neighbor calls to ask if you will bake cookies for the PTA bake sale. You haven't time to bake for your own family, much less for the PTA, but you hesitate a moment, then say "Yes."

Your husband asks you to drop his suit off at the cleaners. He passes it on his way to work and you're late already. But you say "Yes," then seethe inside all the way to the office.

It's never easy to say no, and it can be especially difficult for a working woman with a family, says David Travland, a clinical psychologist who maintains a private practice and works with a large southeastern management consultant firm.

"It's hard to say no because we all want to be liked; we're afraid of being disliked. And people (especially women) have been brainwashed not to think of themselves first," he said.

We grew up thinking self-sacrifice was noble. We watched the women around us devote all their time to caring for others more than themselves.

"Now, women are a bit uneasy because they're no longer following the stereotype. They're working, not devoting all their time to caring for a family. They're uncertain as to what is expected of them in terms of being a 'good' wife or mother," Travland said.

So, sometimes, we say "yes" because we feel guilty, or because we're afraid we'll be disliked, or because we just can't think how to say "no" gracefully.

The result? We tend to spread ourselves too thin. We're exhausted and resentful—and it's our families who will bear the brunt of it in the long run.

"There's nothing wrong with being selfish; that's the first thing we have to realize. If we serve our own best interests, we're often serving the best interests of those around us.

"If we look after our own long-term interests, we make arrangements in our life that keep us comfortable—and the people around us will be more comfortable, too," Travland said.

"It is not only our right, but our obligation to say 'no' if that's in our own best interests," he added. And it will be easier to say "no" if we have set concrete goals for ourselves.

"If there are no goals, there are no priorities. If you have no priorities, you have no basis for saying 'no.' So you end up saying 'yes' by default," Travland said.

If you know at the beginning of the week what you want to accomplish by the end of it, you'll know if you have time to bake cookies, for example.

And once we set priorities for ourselves, once we learn to say "no" if that's in our own best interest, we should no longer resent the request itself.

173

"If you can say 'no,' the request is no longer a threat—so why resent it? You can just say, 'I understand why you might ask that. However, I don't have the time right now.'

"If you feel guilty saying no, say it. Tell them you feel a little guilty, but you're going to say 'no' anyway," Travland said.

It takes practice, he admits. But unless we set priorities, unless we learn to say no when it's in our own best interests, we run the risk of swallowing resentment that may come out later.

"A woman's honesty is crucial to the integrity of any relationship. She is not tied to a particular relationship, but she is tied to herself," Travland said.

"And learning to say 'no' simply means not depending on other people liking you to like yourself."

24

"Is This Bringing Anyone Real Pleasure?"

Christmas is two weeks away—a fact you'd probably just as soon forget. For many working women those weeks will be the most difficult ones in the year.

The days have begun to fly by, each one seemingly shorter than the one before, each leaving us more tense and harassed if we're not careful.

Christmas shopping, entertaining, decorating, baking and coping cheerfully with children who are keyed up, too, can leave us totally exhausted, unless we take some precautions.

One of them is to set realistic goals for ourselves during the holiday season, said a family counselor.

"And that's not easy, because our fantasies get in the way. Everyone tends to fantasize around this time of year. We remember (or think we remember) what Christmas used to be like and we try to duplicate that memory," he said.

"If Mama baked pies and cookies, daughter probably will too. If decorations were lavish, we decorate lavishly.

If presents were always homemade, we feel guilty buying them. And if the holiday season meant two weeks of continuous open house, we entertain a great deal, too."

The only problem with all that is not being *able* to do things quite the way Mama did—especially if Mama didn't have a job away from home. Most working women can't.

It took two Christmases as a working woman for me to realize I simply could not prepare for the holidays as I did when I stayed home full time. They were complete disasters—not because I worked, but because I expected too much of myself.

Determined to go on baking cookies, entertaining, decorating every inch of the house, making Christmas presents and sending cards to everyone I could think of, by Christmas morning *this* working woman was a good deal less than jolly.

"Children will quickly forget whether or not the cookies were homemade—but they're not as likely to forget that mother was irritable and depressed at Christmas time," the counselor said.

He suggested all of us take stock right now, sit down and make a list of priorities.

"It's a matter of deciding what is really important, and that varies with each individual. If homemade cookies are crucial, fine. If making your own presents is important, do it. If you have to entertain for it to seem like Christmas, entertain away. But don't do it all—eliminate what you can," he said.

"Ask yourself 'Is this bringing anyone real pleasure, or am I just doing it because I think I should?' "

The time before Christmas morning can either be calm, relaxed and pleasant for the whole family, or frantic and disjointed as we try to have an old-fashioned Christmas with new-fashioned demands placed on us.

The Christmas card version of Christmas has little to do with the way life really is for most modern, working women. But the joy that is Christmas comes from inside, anyway. If we can get the knots out of our insides, that joy might just have a fighting chance.

Most of the working mothers I know, without full-time housekeepers, have decidedly mixed feelings about Christmastime. The holiday itself is fine, but a ten-day or two-week vacation from school is enough to make them stop believing in Santa Claus.

"It's vacation time; I know how important that is to kids. It's supposed to mean staying up late and having friends over and going to holiday movies and playing with all the new toys, and all that.

"But it can't mean any of that for my kids," a young mother said.

"They are seven and nine years old—certainly not ready to stay home alone. They go to a neighbor's house after school and on most holidays. Generally, they go happily. She has kids just their ages and they play well together.

"But how do you tell kids they can't watch any of the children's specials on television because they have to get up at 6:30 in the morning so Mom can get to work? And how do you tell them, two days after Christmas, that they have to leave all their brand-new toys at home and go somewhere else?

177

"It breaks my heart—they don't really get a Christmas vacation, because I don't," she said.

Mothers of older children have problems too, around this time of year.

"My kids can stay up late and sleep late—very important during vacations when you're in junior high school. But they cannot have friends over when I'm not home. The weather in Indiana this time of year is not exactly conducive to playing outside or meeting friends at a playground. So basically they're stuck in the house together most of the time," said one.

"By about three days after Christmas they'll be fighting and bickering, bored and lonely. And by the end of the first week of vacation, they'll be looking forward to school starting again almost as much as I will."

Solutions? One may be to check local high schools and colleges for a mature student who might be glad for a chance to earn some extra money by babysitting in your home on a temporary basis. Guidance counselors and personnel offices are a good place to start.

Of course you'll ask for references and check them, work out in advance what their duties would be, whether or not they would provide their own transportation, whether or not you would allow them to have company while they're on the job, and what a fair, two-week salary would be.

"I've had the same college girl come and stay with the children during Christmas vacation for four years, now," a mother in Philadelphia said. "She's a day-student and doesn't live far from here. She needs the money, gets bored on vacations anyway, and she makes Christmas a special time for the kids."

You may not get the sort of housekeeping expertise you would expect from an adult. But if your children can stay home with new toys, have friends over to play and generally enjoy this most important vacation—you may be more than willing to ignore a bit of a mess for a little while.

And a good many working mothers hold back a few presents Christmas morning to be given throughout the vacation at regular intervals.

"They don't have to be big gifts. A book, a puzzle, a game that's fun, a record they've been wanting—I save a few of those kinds of presents, wrap them and leave one for each child before I go to work every two or three days," a mother of four said.

"Just having something new—a surprise—is exciting for the children. It makes the whole vacation more fun for all of us, even though I can't be with them during the day," she said.

"Furthermore, I think they appreciate each gift more when they're spread out over a period of time."

For those who are alone, Christmas is surely the loneliest time of the year. Those who are single and far from home, those who are divorced or widowed, ache as they watch friends and coworkers prepare for that most family-oriented of all holidays.

In an office in a city in the South, last year, one working woman decided to do something about those around her who would be alone on Christmas Day.

"I can't take away all the loneliness. But maybe I can make it easier for a few people," she said.

Single and too far away from home, she knew what solitary Christmases were like. So weeks before the big

179

day, she asked several coworkers if they might like to come to her house for Christmas dinner.

"That's really nice, but I think maybe I'll get home this year," one said.

"How nice! But I think the girl I'm dating will be coming over," said another.

"Gee that's a terrific idea—I'll let you know," said a third, vaguely.

It seemed no one in the office needed her company, no one was as alone as she. She felt a bit foolish. And more alone than ever.

Then, the day before Christmas Eve, the coworkers who had planned to go home stopped her in the hall. And the friend whose date was coming over stopped her in the lunch room.

"The plans have kind of fallen through and if the offer is still good, I'd love to drop by Christmas Day," the first said.

"The girl I'm dating is going home for Christmas after all—would you mind if I dropped by?" said the second.

Mind? She was ecstatic. And before the day was over, several other men and women had been offered (and readily accepted) invitations to spend Christmas at her house.

It wasn't quite like home. The turkey was overdone. Three people brought potatoes and no one brought cranberry sauce. There were three pumpkin pies and no mince. Some ate with spoons because the forks gave out.

But there were Christmas carols, candles, and lights twinkling on a tree. There was warmth and laughter, gentleness and love in that house, Christmas Day. For that one day, coworkers become friends and lonely people found companionship.

The day ended (only three dishes and a glass broken) and the next morning it was business as usual. But she vowed to do it again this year. "It was the nicest Christmas I've had in a long time," she said.

This year, plans were being made as early as a month ago for Sally's Christmas. This year, a young single mother and her three small children will join the party.

"I guess in just about any office there are some people who will be alone on Christmas. But not around here—not any more," she laughed.

Something tells me Sally will have a joyful holiday this year.

Niki Scott is the author of the nationally syndicated column, "Working Woman," which appears biweekly in 200 newspapers in the United States and Canada. Until recently, Ms. Scott was a reporter for the *Charlotte (N.C.) News* and, while employed there, won many journalism awards for her feature stories. She recently quit her job and moved to Maine with her family to devote her fulltime attention to freelance writing.

She is especially qualified to write such a book. She has been a fulltime housewife, a part-time working mother, and at one time, a single parent working fulltime to support her two sons.